EVERYDAY CREATIVE WRITING

EVERYDAY
CREATIVE
WRITING

PANNING FOR GOLD
IN THE KITCHEN SINK

MICHAEL C. SMITH
CALIFORNIA STATE UNIVERSITY, LONG BEACH

SUZANNE GREENBERG
CALIFORNIA STATE UNIVERSITY, LONG BEACH

 NTC *Publishing Group*
Lincolnwood, Illinois USA

Executive Editor: John T. Nolan
Sponsoring Editor: Marisa L. L'Heureux
Cover and interior design: Ellen Pettengell
Production Manager: Rosemary Dolinski

ISBN 0-8442-5900-4 (student text)
ISBN 0-8442-5901-2 (instructor's edition)

Published by NTC Publishing Group
© 1996 NTC Publishing Group, 4255 West Touhy Avenue
Lincolnwood (Chicago), Illinois 60646-1975 U.S.A.
Manufactured in the United States of America.
Library of Congress Catalog Card Number: 94-80053

FOR JOEL, WHO ALWAYS GLITTERS

PREFACE

Have you ever seen a movie or read a biography about a writer's wildly adventurous and unconventional life and sighed in weary envy as the credits rolled or you turned the last page? Maybe you went away hopeful and even inspired about writing yourself, and it wasn't until the next day that the predictability of your own life hit you. Perhaps it happened while you were taking the same route to work that you take every morning or doing the coupon math in the supermarket after work or washing dishes while your kids fought over who guessed the phrase first on *Wheel of Fortune*.

The truth is that this is the kind of life that most of us live, writers included. Sure, there are exceptions. A few writers have grants that fund their writing and allow them to pursue their craft in a leisurely fashion while looking out a window in an Italian villa. But only a small number of writers make enough money by writing to work full-time at it. Most are forced by the necessities of economics to have a "real" job, too, or, by the necessity of their circumstances, to raise children or care for older relatives. *Everyday Creating Writing: Panning for Gold in the Kitchen Sink* is a book that presumes that the life you are living now *is already* the writer's life. We believe that inspiring ideas can be found in the everyday, even in the murky soap bubbles in the kitchen sink, and the exercises in this book are designed to lead you to those ideas.

The book gets the first part of its title from one of possibly an infinite number of metaphors for the writer: that of being a prospector, a forty-niner, who continues the search for gold long after the main veins have been tapped and after everyone has given up. What this prospector discovers is that the plain rocks and jackrabbit bones usually discarded have their own luster and that virtually anything that we encounter can be valuable once touched with our efforts and marked with our individual signature.

Creative writing is too often seen as the *exclusive* preserve of university writing programs, and there's no denying that extensive reading and institutions of higher learning can provide the material and context in which creative writing can be understood in a fuller historical and critical way. But whether or not they are affiliated with writing programs, many people still play with words, spin yarns, write amusing anecdotes. People who write creatively do so for the same reasons that others sing or dance or play instruments or paint: to express something of their true selves; to reflect on what they did, thought, or felt; to capture evanescent truths or produce moments of beauty—and sometimes just to let others know that they were here.

Modern psychology and self-help movements perhaps exaggerate the importance of our knowing ourselves, but we believe that in the world of creative writing, it is not an exaggeration to say that the genuine is the individual. Provide others with your unique take on the world, your own angle, your imaginative fingerprint or DNA code, and you have provided a gift more valuable than gold. The exercises in this book are designed to help you extract that gift. They give you hundreds of sites in which to dig for your life and recover previous ore.

This is a book of writing exercises for students, teachers, and writers, whether they are professional or amateur, beginning or advanced, committed or dabbling; anyone who wants to write something creative but can't quite get started, has temporary writer's block, or simply enjoys a new challenge will enjoy this book. It is a book for those who sometimes prefer to *do* rather than to think and read about doing. We believe that what distinguishes writers from other sorts of people is that, first and foremost, writers write. If you complete these exercises, regardless of how you complete them and regardless of the quality or merits of the results, you will be doing what creative writers do.

ACKNOWLEDGMENTS

We received support from many colleagues and friends as we worked on this project. We wish, first, to thank our reviewers: Allen Woodman, Northern Arizona University; Art Homer, the Writer's Workshop, University of Nebraska at Omaha; and Patricia Bridges, Mount Union College. We are grateful for the valuable advice they offered us as we worked toward our final draft.

Special thanks go to *all* our family and friends who put up with us this past year—in particular, Gina Sawin, who patiently encouraged us to talk our way through this book before it was a book; Cornel Bonca and Jan Fehrman, whose long-distance phone consultations helped to keep us sane early on; Joyce and Gary Lott, who offered us their support and expertise; and Larry Greenberg, Gina Caruso, and Sarah Michaelson, who have unfailingly believed in the strength of our ideas and words.

We are supremely indebted to our editor, Marisa L. L'Heureux, who promised she would work with us from start to finish and kept her word. We quickly came to count on her gentle, reasonable counsel and astute observations at important stages in our writing and editing processes, as well as her sense of perspective and humor.

Finally, we wish to thank our students at Howard University, the University of Maryland, Bowie State University, and the Maryland-National Park and Planning Commission, whose creative energies demanded so much new material from us each week that they left us no choice but to finally write a book.

CONTENTS

PREFACE   vii

INTRODUCTION   xiii

 PROVISIONS AND PROSPECTING TOOLS   1

PROVISIONS   2

Optional Provisions   8

PROSPECTING TOOLS   8

Freewriting   8
Brainstorming   10
Listing   11
Clustering   12
Free Association   12
Puzzles, Games, and Computers   14
Using Your Computer   16
Resistance as a Tool   17
Using a Combination of Tools   19

FROM NUGGETS TO ARTIFACTS: WHAT FORM SHOULD YOU CHOOSE?   20

Consider Writing a Poem from an Exercise If   21
Consider Writing a Story from an Exercise If   22
Consider Writing an Essay from an Exercise If   22

AROUND THE HOUSE   25

WHY I WILL NOT GET OUT OF BED   26

HOLDING ON AND LETTING GO   30

PARTY INVITATIONS   34

BAGGAGE   38

AT THE DINNER TABLE   43

PAPER TRAILS   47

DANCING WITH DAD   50

THE SPICE RACK   54

THE ELEMENTS   58

THE EVOLUTION OF MINI-SKILLS   62

THE NOTE READ, "THERE ARE MORE WHERE THESE CAME FROM"   66

QUILTING   69

THE FAMILY NORMAL   73

PHOTO ALBUM   78

PRODUCT WARNINGS   82

 DOWN THE STREET   87

GETTING LOST, FINDING THE WAY   88

EFFECTS AND SIDE EFFECTS   92

CAUGHT UP IN THE NEWS   95

NEIGHBORLY AND UNNEIGHBORLY NEIGHBORS   98

CUSTOMS AND THE CUSTOMARY   102

FIRST TIMES   105

"I Would Have Burned My Hair for That Waitress"   **108**

Community Service   **111**

The Road Not Taken   **115**

The Briefcase   **118**

Around the Water Cooler   **121**

In the Checkout Line   **126**

Why I Hate Vacations   **129**

Modern Romance   **132**

Air Travel: Unlikely Seatmates   **135**

 In the Gold Mine   **139**

Folk Remedies   **140**

The Cliché's the Thing   **144**

Mixing Relationship Boundaries   **148**

What Things Say   **151**

Changes in Preference   **154**

Subtitles and Doubletalk   **157**

"The Marigold Is Like a Stalled School Bus"   **160**

Morphemes   **164**

Creating the Evil Twin   **168**

Character by Association   **173**

"My Mother Was Like an Ornate Castle"   **177**

Returning from the Dead   **180**

As Restless as Pantyhose   **184**

Artful Lying   **188**

Implausible Causes and Unlikely Effects   **191**

ASSAYING: HOW DO YOU KNOW IT'S GOLD? 195

DOES IT GLITTER: FRESHNESS AND ORIGINALITY   197

The Topic or Piece of Writing Keeps Coming Back to You   198
You Find Yourself "Working" on the Piece Without Deliberately Trying
    To   198
The Beginning of the Piece Helped You Discover Something You
    Didn't Know about Yourself or Someone Else or the Human
    Condition   198
You Are Intrigued by an Odd or Original Connection You Have Made
    Between Two Seemingly Very Different Things   199
You Introduced a Character You Like a Great Deal and Are Concerned
    about What Might Happen to Him or Her   199
You Introduced a Character You Dislike and Are Concerned about the
    Damage He or She May Do   199
You Love the Sound of the Words You've Strung Together   200
You Feel Like You Could Write a Lot More about This   200
You're Dying to Send/Show the Piece to Others   201
You Feel That What You've Written Is Fresh or Original   201
You Believe That What You've Written Honestly Expresses Some of
    Your Feelings   202
What You've Written Has Energy   203
You've Created Tension or Conflict   203

HOW TO SORT REAL GOLD FROM FOOL'S GOLD   204

Be Sure That What You've Written Doesn't Descend into
    Cliché   204
Beware of What Too Easily Amuses or Impresses You   206

SOME FINAL THOUGHTS   207

FOR FURTHER READING   208

ACKNOWLEDGMENTS   211

INDEX   215

INTRODUCTION

*E*veryday Creative Writing: Panning for Gold in the Kitchen Sink is organized into five sections—**Provisions and Prospecting Tools, Around the House, Down the Street, In the Gold Mine,** and **Assaying: How Do You Know It's Gold?**

The first section, **Provisions and Prospecting Tools,** outfits you with both basic and less common writing equipment: freewriting, brainstorming, free association, listing, and computer gaming, among others. We also include in this section a discussion of how to determine what form—for example, poetry, fiction, or creative nonfiction—your exercise might be best cast in. You may choose to read **Provisions and Prospecting Tools** first, or you may want to dig right into the three middle sections that are the core of the book.

The **Around the House** section includes exercises that use as creative writing resources things, processes, and behaviors with which you are intimately familiar, including your family, chores, and routines. The **Down the Street** section exploits your experiences with the outside world, including work, travel, and romance. And the **In the Gold Mine** section gathers creative writing exercises that make use of abstract ideas, fantasies, dreams, emotions, lies, promises, play, and pure speculation. All these exercises work equally well with poetry, fiction, or creative nonfiction (we use the terms *creative nonfiction* and *essay* interchangeably to mean prose writing that is significantly fact-based).

The final section of the book, **Assaying: How Do You Know It's Gold?,** provides some suggestions for how to evaluate what you've found in your digging in order to help you identify the work that might be worth further development and refinement.

Each exercise in the middle three sections contains background and instructions for getting started on two different levels, what we call "Panning Instructions" and "Excavating Instructions." In many cases, but not in all, the "Excavating Instructions" ask you to go "deeper" into your material. For example, in the "Getting Lost and Finding the Way" exercise, the "Panning Instructions" relate to getting actually and geographically lost, while the "Excavating Instructions" ask you to explore situations where you couldn't find your way emotionally, logically, or spiritually. In some cases, the two sets of instructions simply address different angles on the same subject. Read over both sets of instructions before you begin, and choose the set that inspires you the most at the moment.

We give examples of *actual outcomes*—what we call **Nuggets**—for each exercise. And we also include examples of published work—what we call **Artifacts**—that relate in some way to the exercises. Some of our exercises grew out of these published pieces; sometimes the published works were incorporated because they illustrate some aspect of the exercise or generally relate to the exercise's subject.

The exercises ask you to explore a variety of topics drawn largely from everyday life, and in most cases the exercises suggest specific approaches to the topics. However, you will undoubtedly veer away from the topics and approaches suggested to pursue your own ideas and inclinations. Ultimately, there may be very little similarity between what the exercise instructions ask for and what you have written, *and that's fine.* To derive the greatest benefit from this book, while you are doing the exercises, you should remain open to all the possibilities generated and suggested by your own imagination, even if this takes you away from the exercises. It will help to maintain a sense of serious playfulness throughout, an attitude not so oppressively serious that your responses get predictable, nor so wildly fun-loving that only silliness is possible. While we have tried to provide detailed instructions for the completion of each exercise, as long as you are writing something, there is no "correct" or "incorrect." The book's primary objective—and our greatest hope—is that in doing the exercises, you will get caught up in the interplay between your imagination and the act of writing.

Regardless of your ultimate writing goals—publication, self-expression, and so forth—we recommend that you use this book as a way of jumping directly into writing when you don't have any particular form (story, poem, essay) or subject in mind. All you need to know is that you want to write something of a creative nature. If you're not familiar with the prewriting tools we describe in the **Provisions and Prospecting Tools** section, such as freewriting, brainstorming, listing, and clustering, you might want to familiarize yourself with these first. Alternatively, you can just pick any exercise in any of the three exercise sections, get started on it, and if a writing tool with which you are not familiar is mentioned—the terms for these are printed in **bold**—go back to **Provisions and Prospecting Tools** and learn what it is and how to use it.

We believe that the act of writing itself will ultimately suggest what form your beginning efforts should lead to. If you are not particularly familiar with poetry, fiction, or creative nonfiction, the last part of the **Provisions and Prospecting Tools** section—"From Nuggets to Artifacts: What Form Should You Choose?"—should help you decide whether you should work on a story, a poem, or a piece of creative nonfiction.

You can read this book from cover to cover and complete each exercise in the order presented—which we would love and which would result in an incredible amount of material. You may be using the book in a creative writing class in which specific exercises are assigned and discussed on a schedule, or you might use it as a source of group challenges in one of the thousands of writing groups that have sprung up over the last few years. You may be using it as a lone writer in search of just a few notions to get you started; you might, from time to time, skim the text and light on an exercise or an aspect of an exercise that inspires you. There is no right or wrong way of using this book so long as the result is writing.

What this book *does not do* is offer specific instruction in the techniques of writing poetry, fiction, or creative nonfiction. There are a lot of books that already do this very well, and for those who are interested in this kind of guidance, we recommend some specific texts in the **For Further Reading** section at the end of the book. In addition, many writers learn technique through reading, and we hope that some of these exercises inspire you not only to write, but to search out more work by the published writers we introduce you to in each section.

Where you go from here is up to you. Gold can be cast into many forms: delicate chains, durable wedding bands, and even magical chalices. Some of these exercises may yield nuggets beautiful in their own right, while others may benefit from further shaping and forming. Wherever these exercises lead you, we hope you enjoy the prospecting itself.

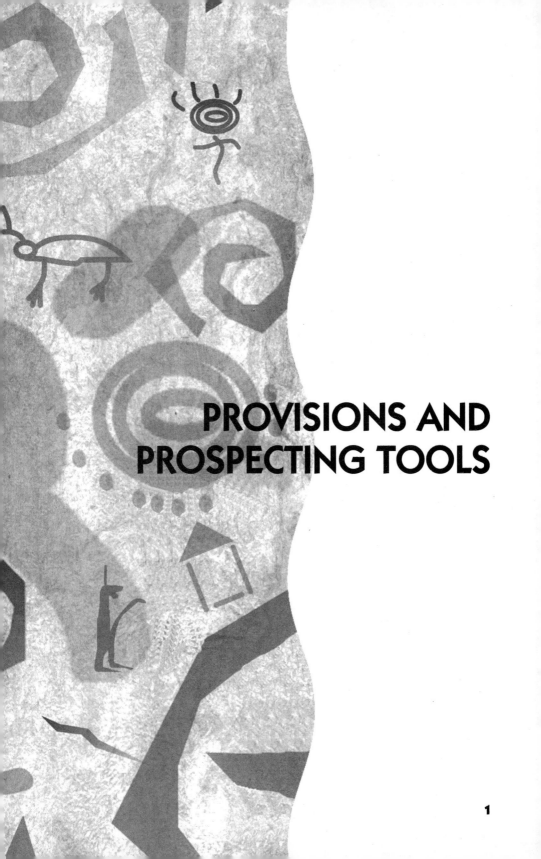

PROVISIONS AND PROSPECTING TOOLS

Y ou might think that all a writer really needs to get started are a few blank sheets of paper and a couple of durable pens. Technically, you'd be right. While a scuba diver, skier or bungee jumper has to buy or rent elaborate, expensive equipment, many excellent poems, stories, novels, and essays have been written longhand by people with meager incomes and serious misgivings about technology. Writers need rich imaginations more than they need padded bank accounts or elaborate machines. Of course, having use of a computer or word processor is a bonus—more on that later—but many of the provisions and tools you'll need most as you start off on your journey are far less tangible than a color monitor or hard drive.

Some of the most successful early Argonauts—gold seekers—brought little more on their quests than a tin wash pan in which to separate gold from earth, while others felt more comfortable outfitting themselves like L. L. Bean models. Ultimately what you take with you, what *you* absolutely need, depends on you and, to a certain degree, on your experience as a writer. The following are suggestions.

PROVISIONS

We recommend that in addition to writing implements—pens, typewriter, etc.—you include a loose-leaf notebook for doing the exercises and a bound notebook to serve as a **logbook** for recording your reactions and experiences as you do the exercises. These are by no means essential, and if acquiring them or using them deters you in any way, leave them behind. You may find later, however, that you would like a more organized and systematic way of dealing with the exercises and the notebook and logbook can do this.

Use the **logbook** to record your efforts to complete the exercises, as well as your impressions and responses, in the way that some of the early prospectors recorded their prospecting adventures and findings, and the way that scientists record the conditions and outcomes of their experiments and doctors chart their patients' progress and setbacks. By doing this, you force yourself to stand back a little and think about what you've written and how you wrote it. In the long run, this **logbook** may be even more valuable to you than the exercises themselves.

While you can include anything you consider useful in the **logbook,** we suggest that you include the following:

1. Date and time you attempted the exercise.
2. Where you were when you did the exercise.
3. The name of the exercise.
4. The amount of continuous time you spent on the exercise.
5. The outcome of the exercise, including:
   a. Your initial reaction to the exercise after reading it.
   b. Difficulties you encountered in doing the exercise.
   c. Discoveries you made while doing the exercise.
   d. Ideas that occurred to you for further writing.

Items 1–4 are not particularly important, but recording these items can supply a sense of order, and they're easy enough to jot down. Item 5 is the crux of the logbook, and completing this item may take you even longer than completing the exercise.

The following illustrates a student's work on an exercise from the **Around the House** section of the book and his reaction in his **logbook** to that work and to the exercise itself:

DAVE'S START ON "BAGGAGE" EXERCISE

Around the time I was ten, my mother asked me to pack for myself for a family trip up the coast. Early into the second day it became apparent that I had left behind all but one pair of underwear in the top drawer back home. How come we didn't make a detour to do some underwear shopping, I don't know. Each evening before bed I took off my size 22 J.C. Penney briefs to air them by the window. My brother and visiting cousin thought this was pretty funny. They didn't pack for themselves . . . yet. Underwear always tops my list for things to bring on vacation. . . .

DAVE'S LOGBOOK ENTRY

Date/Time:	*July 19, 1994, 5:00 P.M.*
Place:	*Duck, NC*
Name of Exercise:	*"Baggage"*
Amount of Time:	*About Thirty Minutes*

Outcomes:

Reactions/Responses to Doing the Exercise:
I need more thoughts into spinning a metaphor out of forgetting underwear. I like the voice in baggage.

Difficulties:
Couldn't get going on the Excavating part of the exercise. I can't really remember much emotion with my trip—do I make it up?

Discoveries:
I don't like looking for psychological baggage.

Ideas for Further Writing:
1. *The nagging feeling one experiences before leaving that something is left behind.*
2. *Why do I usually take so much underwear on a trip?*
3. *Taking a road-trip with brother and cousin and the dynamics between the three of us and the parents.*

The following student worked on several exercises from **Around the House** for an hour and decided to react to all three of them together in the log sheet that follows his starts:

MIKE'S START ON "PARTY INVITATIONS" EXERCISE

Come Celebrate:	*One smoke-free year*
Time:	*9:00 P.M. The time I used to be on the deck having that after-dinner smoke.*
Place:	*Our house, where no one has smoked in three years. I started smoking on the deck in the rain, sleet, or snow, when we found out Mad was pregnant.*
Bring:	*Food—my appetite has improved*
Wear:	*Anything you want a cigarette hole burned in as you brush by someone on the way to the kitchen*

MIKE'S START ON "THE NOTE READ, 'THERE ARE MORE WHERE THESE CAME FROM'"

Mad,
> *Went to the playground; back in a half-hour.*
> > *8:00, Mike*

Mad,

Money is on the coffee table. You are on empty. Sorry, I had to rush home with ice cream.

Call me, Mike

Mad,

Where are the August Safeway coupons? Check #861—Who and how much? Who's got Max tonight?

Mike

Mad,

While you were out, all of your friends called. They are all having serious crises that require long telephone conversations. They all want you to call back immediately.

Mike

MIKE'S START ON "PRODUCT WARNINGS"

Common Warnings:

*   *Harmful if swallowed*

*   *Use only in well-ventilated areas*

*   *The Surgeon General has determined that smoking is dangerous to your health*

*   *Smoking by pregnant women may cause low birth weight*

*   *Induce vomiting if swallowed*

New Combinations:

*   *Swallowing may induce vomiting in pregnant women*

MIKE'S LOGBOOK ENTRY

Date/Time:	*June 8, 1994, 3–4 p.m.*
Place:	*Deli Parking Lot/In Car*
Name of Exercise:	*"Party Invitations," "The Note Read . . ." and "Product Warnings"*
Amount of Time:	*One Hour*
Outcomes:	

Reactions/Responses to Doing the Exercise:
I enjoyed them—which surprised me.

Difficulties:
I found it difficult to get started and to keep going, but I did.

Discoveries:
I am creatively stunted and need serious work—ha!

Ideas for Further Writing:
Product Warnings for major life decisions. How would these be given? Would you have to sign off that you had received the warnings? Would you then be prohibited from later complaining about your car, wife, career, etc.?

As you can see from these first two logbook entries, there's no right or wrong way to keep a logbook. Although both Dave and Mike are beginning writers, Dave may be taking his writing more seriously at this point than Mike takes his. Yet each of them has made some interesting and potentially useful comments that may help them develop as writers. Dave feels pleased with the "voice" in this piece, but is beginning to question his unwillingness to examine psychological and emotional areas in his writing. Mike may seem to laugh off or dismiss the work he has done, but he does allow himself to admit he enjoyed writing—an important impetus for doing more—and he comes up with an intriguing idea for another piece.

The next exercise start and sample logbook entry were completed by a writer with somewhat more experience than either Dave or Mike:

Toni's Start on "At the Dinner Table"

"Dinner's ready, everyone!" my mother yelled out from the kitchen.

"Oh, joy," my brother said, turning the page of the detective novel he was reading.

"That means you, too, mister!" my mother yelled as if she could see him still lying there.

I put one more piece in the puzzle I was putting together—the cherry on the top of an ice-cream sundae two smiling teenage girls were sharing— and stepped back from the card table to survey my work. I had done this puzzle at least twenty times since I bought it with my allowance money two weeks before, but each time I put it together, the world in it that I had assembled seemed new and almost magical.

"Let's go, secret agent No. 14," my brother said, up from the couch now and nudging me toward the dining room where, per usual, we'd find our stepfather sitting at the head of the table waiting for my mother to serve him.

I took my place quietly and watched as my mother heaped spoonfuls of the creamy tuna noodle casserole she had made on his plate. This was a new recipe. We found it in one of her magazines earlier in the day, and I knew she was nervous about whether he would like it. Some of the ingredients—crunchy onion bits and angel hair noodles, for example—were pretty exotic, at least as far as our household was concerned.

I could see that none of us were going to get served until he tried it. I thought of the ice-cream sundae I was building in the other room, listened to my brother clear his throat suggestively, and concentrated on not letting my stomach growl. Slowly my stepfather's fork made its way to his plate. The only thing I disliked more than watching him eat was waiting for him to begin. Then he put down his fork and adjusted his water glass while we all waited. . . .

TONI'S LOGBOOK ENTRY

Date/Time: *March 3, 1994, 1:30 P.M.*
Place: *Ledo's Pizza Place*
Name of Exercise: *"At the Dinner Table"*
Amount of Time: *45 Minutes*
Outcomes:

Reactions/Responses to Doing the Exercise:
I thought this was going to be a tough exercise because I couldn't immediately remember any particular family meal. They all kind of blurred together.

Difficulties:
It took me a long time (about 10 minutes) to get an angle on the exercise before I could really start writing.

Discoveries:
I finally suddenly remembered this meal that I just knew was absolutely typical of all our meals together. I remembered that my stepfather never cooked—never even washed a dish—and it kind of irritated me to think about him.

Ideas for Further Writing:
I think it would be interesting to imagine my stepfather actually trying to prepare a meal for my brother and myself—from our point of view at that age. Maybe I could write a truly fictional piece where I focused on his awkwardness as a chef. It's hard even to imagine him setting the table— the slim silverware in those big awkward hands of his.

Your own log entries may be as detailed and analytical as Toni's, or they may be shorter, like Dave's or Mike's. Our experience has been that the more writers *write*, the more developed their logbook journal entries become. But, as we have seen, even shorter, early entries can provide a novice writer with valuable clues for future exploration.

Optional Provisions

Many writers and other creative people also use **journals** to jot down ideas and observations, as well as **diaries** to record reflections and experiences, and these can serve as valuable sources of material for stories, poems, and essays. Some writers also find it useful to keep several **notecards** around for moments of inspiration. In addition to being very portable (they fit in a shirt pocket or wallet), notecards can be organized in a variety of ways, including by color.

PROSPECTING TOOLS

Beyond a desire to write and a willingness to freely explore your imagination, all that you need to get started are a few simple prospecting tools to help you dislodge material from your imagination—the picks, shovels, and sluice boxes of the writing process. Many of the tools we describe in this section perform basically the same function: they loosen up or shake up or knock down material from memory and imagination, in a fashion similar to how picks, shovels, and dynamite are used. The idea with these tools, and with this entire book, is to free up your thinking processes and imagination. No claim we make in this book is any more certain than the claim that you have within you 24-karat experiences, memories, and imaginings. Which tools you use to get at this gold is simply a matter of what you and your sensibility feel most comfortable using. While some of the exercises will prompt you to use specific tools (these will be highlighted in **bold**), we suggest that you at least try them all once or twice in the course of completing the exercises. As anyone who has used tools knows, the right tool can make the difference between a day and a week.

Freewriting

As the name of this technique suggests, **freewriting** is a way of freely jotting down whatever occurs to you. At its freest, freewriting is simply writing anything and everything that comes to mind with no regard for meaning, significance, or topic. The point of doing this is to allow your unconscious to pour into your writing with all its beauty, uniqueness, and wildness. Variations on freewriting make it less free but perhaps more effective for certain situations.

Timed freewriting simply imposes a time period for the freewriting, say five to ten minutes. During this period, you should write continuously, again without regard to what you are writing. If you can't think of anything and are about to stop, simply repeat the last thing you wrote or repeat a phrase you used before, for example "I'm thinking about, I'm thinking about, I'm thinking about" or "I can't think, I can't think, I can't think," until you come up with something else. The idea is just to write continuously for a period of time you prescribe for yourself. The following is an example of two minutes of timed freewriting:

> *freewriting freewriting what's free about freewriting pencils? pencils are cheap who uses a pencil anymore? can't think of anything can't think of anything except the smell of pencil shavings the way it takes me back to grade school fond memories but which ones specifically something about pencil shavings that smell the smell of promise the unopened box of crayons the new notebooks such hopeful things but by the second week everything's written in tattered the crayons broken the compass and scissors lost pencil shavings do that to me can't think of anything can't think of anything except the Mets what about the Mets? who cares I don't know much about baseball except it makes me tense the psychology of pitchers and batters the waiting the waiting and scratching waiting and scratching what an image adults do this waiting and scratching.*

Focused freewriting takes off on specific words or ideas and returns to the words or ideas periodically. Again the idea is to write continuously without evaluation, but in this case with some effort to generally focus on a topic, subject, or theme. With focused freewriting, you may digress or take off from your topic as long as your digression is interesting to you; however, when you run out of things to say about the digression, return to the words or ideas you started with. The following illustrates how focused freewriting can move back and forth from the concept of "vacations":

VACATIONS

> *Time away from something less than completely desirable. I remember our vacations to the lake—Lake Mohawk . . . a very green lake that used to be called Lake Cow but was renamed for marketing purposes. Wanted to attract more kids. The great thing about Lake Mohawk was that it had a high water slide and a pier in the middle also a long rope that swung out over the water. The first time I swung out and dropped into that water I was shocked first by how cold it was and then by how deep I'd fallen. Didn't know which way was up and at first swam down thinking it was up and realized in panic . . . Vacations are times spent in alternative realities. Shakespeare's characters had important revelations in the woods, which were always enchanted. Vacation. Vacate. Make empty. To vacate a building. Motel vacancy. To vacate our senses. A vacation from sense. A vacation from despair . . . Vacant.*

Notice how the writer of the above example allows herself to explore how Lake Mohawk got its name and to even bring in Shakespeare's romances and how, finally, she brings the freewriting back to the concept and meaning of "vacation."

Freewriting can be used at any stage of the writing process to shake loose material in your memory and imagination. It can be used alone or in combination with the other techniques we're about to discuss.

Brainstorming

You may already be familiar with this writing tool as a problem-solving technique used in many other contexts. What **brainstorming** shares with freewriting and other techniques we will discuss is, again, the absence of self-judgment or evaluation. Brainstorming works best when used in conjunction with specific prompt questions. In the initial stages of a typical problem-solving situation, a question related to the problem is posed and solutions are solicited. All solutions—even the wildest and most bizarre—are tentatively accepted and recorded. After all conceivable solutions have been provided, then, and only then, should evaluation of each suggestion begin. As a simple example, let's say your back door tends to swing in the wind because the latch doesn't work. Brainstorming among members of the family, the following creative solutions are offered:

1. Use a bungee cord to hold it closed.
2. Call the locksmith.
3. Use two huge magnets.
4. Strap it back with nylon stockings.
5. Take off the door.
6. Block the wind.
7. Have somebody stand there and hold it closed.
8. Stick gerbils under the door.
9. Invite neighbors over for a door-closing party.
10. Pile recyclables in front of the door.

While the above example of brainstorming involves solutions to a material problem, this same technique can be used in writing to generate and explore ideas. Imagine writing about a couple of the unlikely solutions listed above, not in an effort to solve a material problem but as a way of getting started:

IDEA FOR A STORY

The door was held open by a pair of nylon stockings. Something was definitely wrong. She was sitting in the kitchen drinking a Coke and twirling a pair of scissors the way cowboys used to twirl their Colt 45s. . . .

IDEA FOR AN ESSAY

The mechanical world and I have had a testy relationship. When things break, I tend to get emotional, and the mechanical world couldn't care less. I got so frustrated with the door that kept banging open and closed despite my efforts to make it stop that I called all my neighbors and told them to come over. I told them I was having a party, a party just to celebrate that door, that damned wonderful door. My best friends understood; the door, I suspect, didn't.

IDEA FOR A POEM

*The back door bangs shut
as often as it swings open
but the latter I hear, the latter
unnerves. I tie it closed
with a pair of nylon stockings.
The new silence also
unnerves as crisp as something
unearned. . . .*

Listing

In some ways very similar to freewriting and brainstorming, **listing** is a popular and fun way of establishing categories and filling them with creative examples.

The listing activity uses questions, prompts, or categories, either given or created, to generate items both predictable and surprising, tame and wild, colorful and drab. Listing provides an inviting structure within which creative momentum can mount and produce some surprising results, as the following student example illustrates:

Prompt: Reasons I never wear green

1. It clashes with my eyes.
2. I blend in with the grass.
3. I feel like a clown.
4. I'm often mistaken for an after-dinner mint.
5. It reminds me of the money I don't have.
6. It clashes with my eyes.
7. I look like I'm dead.

8.   I faint.

9.   It makes me feel Irish.

10.   It suggests that I lack experience.

11.   I feel like a clown.

12.   Everything I eat tastes like lime.

13.   It's the color of my ex-husband's Jaguar.

14.   It clashes with my eyes.

15.   None of my perfumes match.

Notice that this writer repeats ideas when she feels momentarily stuck for something new. We suggest listing in several exercises and supply prompts and questions to help you get started. You should also consider using lists in exercises that don't specifically ask for them, if the material seems suitable.

Clustering

For those who are more visually oriented and who like to draw and doodle, **clustering** may be a very productive writing tool (see the example on page 13). Invented by Gabriele Lusser Rico, the author of *Writing the Natural Way,* clustering involves drawing circles around words and phrases and connecting them to other circles with related words and phrases. This is a very intuitive and recursive process that shows you how ideas branch and grow and permutate. The sample creates a cluster from the word *green,* the subject of the last exercise.

Notice how each balloon in the cluster becomes the beginning or nucleus of another cluster. The centers of the clusters and associated clusters can be combined in a variety of ways to begin poems, stories, or essays.

Free Association

Developed and made popular by Freudian psychoanalysts, **free association** is a technique for getting at what Freudians would call repressed material in the unconscious. To free associate means to say the first thing that comes to your mind when presented with a word, a phrase, or an object. Freud discovered that when his patients slipped and said something that sounded like a simple mistake, often the mistake highlighted or pointed to a complex of some kind. This is the origin of the expression "Freudian slip." In writing, this technique can help you generate some surprising material when you keep it up for a few minutes, free associating from one word to the next. When used by an analyst, free association begins with the analyst saying one word and the patient responding immediately with the first word that comes to mind. The analyst then provides another word, and the patient repeats the process with that word and so on. When the patient responds with something significant or unusual, the analyst may stop the free associations to talk about specific responses to see where they lead.

SAMPLE CLUSTER

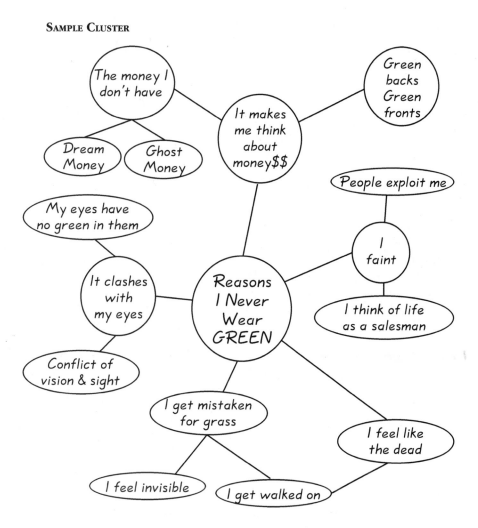

In the context of a writing exercise, there is of course no analyst to supply words; however, free associating in a chain or sequence alone can also have the effect of dredging up surprising material.

For example, let's see where free associating took one student who was just starting on "The Spice Rack" exercise:

garlic blood vodka ice seals walrus whiskers stars broomsticks Kool Aid orange crate slingshot.

Notice how the above sequence of free associations leaps around, at times almost making sense, but ultimately creating a very individual psychic trail. No two people would produce the same sequence. These words, while seemingly unrelated, came from the same mind. The connections remain to be explored and used by the writer. The writer may choose to freewrite or list possible connections between words she has free associated or begin a story, essay, or poem that incorporates several of the words and how they're related.

Puzzles, Games, and Computers

In addition to the tools above that you already possess, there are many other valuable writing tools that themselves use other tools or things or documents that have already been created. The possibilities for generating writing ideas using computer software, for example, are probably limitless, and the last few years have produced many programs aimed specifically at writing and the various steps in the writing process. Word games such as Scrabble, Boggle, Twenty Questions, and Ad Libs can be used directly or can be adapted to help you generate ideas for beginning. The following list of tools is by no means exhaustive, and we encourage you to look for other tools that can help you generate exciting writing ideas.

Puzzling Crosswords.   Even if you don't have a lot of success with that crossword puzzle in the *New York Times,* you can use it or other crossword puzzles to help you generate writing ideas. This technique requires that you give up on "their" solution and use the structure of the puzzle to help you find your solutions.

You can use this tool simply to come up with random words, or you can use it to develop one of the exercises in this book.

To do the latter, simply write the name of the exercise (for example, "Baggage") above any unworked-on crossword puzzle from any source. Next, ignoring the puzzle's clues, simply fill in only the vertical elements or the horizontal elements of the puzzle with words related to the exercise—or any other words—that fit in the spaces. (Do not try to actually use both vertical and horizontal elements to make crosswords. This will drive you nuts, and it's not the point anyway, as you'll see.) Then, simply list all the words you used to fill the blanks in the puzzle, mix and match them, combine and modify them, and use them in the piece you're working on as appropriate. The writer who filled in the crossword puzzle on the following page came up with this start on a story:

> *I was never afraid of flying until I spent four hours sitting next to a drunk pilot. Although he was off-duty, from the way he spit back his beer, I doubted his ability to stay sober anytime. He corrected a number of*

SAMPLE CROSSWORD PUZZLE

AIR TRAVEL: UNLIKELY SEATMATES

STANLEY B. WHITTEN

```
P L A N E   S E A T   B E E R
C A R G O   N U T S   S O D A
S I T B Y   D R U N K P I L O T
M E A L   M A S K   S N O R E
      F A L L   O X Y G E N
G L A S S E S   F E A R
A L O N E   N E R V E   J E T
L A N D   T I R E D   B O O K
L A G   D R U N K   G R O S S
    W I P E   E X P L O D E
  F L I G H T   R E A D
N O S E Y   Y E L L   T A L K
F L Y I N G W I T H A F O O L
S P I T   J E R K   A R G U E
C O O L   M I N T   S P I L L
```

myths about air travel that I would just as soon not have corrected. He told me that if you ever had to use the oxygen mask, it would be too late anyway, that the oxygen mask was there more as a charm, that planes usually explode when they crash and that nothing will save you. "Damn straight," he said, slamming down his beer on his tray so hard that it spilled out at me. "And the cargo's the best place to be in case of turbulence. Your luggage is safer than you are."

What he said caught a nerve in my stomach and I couldn't eat my meal or even read the book I took with me. I ate both of our packets of nuts and drank my soda until the jerk finally started snoring. . . .

Word Strings. Choose one word related to your exercise and write another word beginning with the last letter of the first word that relates to your exercise—however remotely—and keep this up until you've generated at least ten words. For example, let's say you're working on the "Mixing Relationship Boundaries" exercise, and you've chosen to explore your relationship with your brother. You, in fact, begin with the word *brother*:

brother ridiculous selfish hearty youthful lively yearning grouchy yet tame eager relentless sad

More than likely, in the course of completing the string, you will come up with some ideas that might otherwise not have occurred to you. Try to incorporate some of these words and ideas in your initial writing efforts.

Using Your Computer

There are many computer programs on the market now that address the various steps in the writing process. Some packages have prewriting software that allows you to automatically match up nouns and relevant verbs and create idea and word chains. No program can substitute for your memories and imagination, but they can be fun to experiment with. Even if you only have access to word processing software with a dictionary and thesaurus, you can use a computer to generate writing ideas.

Computer Thesaurus.   Choose a word from the title of the exercise or one that you came up with while freewriting, brainstorming, or engaging in one of the other prewriting techniques described in this section, and look it up in the computer thesaurus. Draw up a list of synonyms and antonyms and use them to take you in different directions related to your subject. For example, let's say you're working on the "Why I Hate Vacations" exercise and that you look up the word *vacation* in the thesaurus. The following options appear:

holiday
furlough
leave
respite
sabbatical
break
lull
recess
rest

The concept of military "leave" or "furlough" captures your imagination, so you look those words up in the thesaurus, with the following result:

depart
exit
flee
retreat
embark
enplane
go abroad
weigh anchor
abandon

desert
forsaken
relinquish

You discover that in many of the synonyms, there is the unmistakable sense of "giving up" or "surrendering." It occurs to you that, indeed, a vacation is an admission of defeat in some ways and an effort to flee the enemy before you are killed or driven crazy. This idea could serve as a beginning of an essay, story, or poem. Notice, though, that other synonyms would lead in other directions—for example, the synonym *holiday* carries with it the sense of celebration or festivity, an idea almost the opposite of *surrender*.

You can also use a regular bound thesaurus with this approach, but you may lose some of the fluidity that a computer thesaurus provides.

Computer Dictionary. Purposely misspell any word related to one of the exercises to see what other words your internal computer dictionary comes up with. For example, let's say you are doing "The Spice Rack" exercise and misspell the word *oregano* as "oragano." Our computer dictionary asked us to consider the following options, including the correct spelling of oregano:

Oregon
origin
orogeny
Uruguayan

The unfamiliar word *orogeny* is defined in the dictionary as "the process of mountain making," from the Greek word *orogen,* meaning "back formation." The word *origin* has a similar Latin root that means "to rise, come forth." These remotely related terms and words could be imaginatively incorporated into a description of the flavor of oregano. For example,

The flavor of oregano rises on the palate like a lush tropical mountain. . . .

Resistance as a Tool

For many of you, refraining from judging your initial exploratory writing efforts may be the hardest exercise, and if you find this to be the case, we recommend that you talk back in writing to your inclinations to judge the outcomes of the exercises. Because most of us are accustomed to writing to someone else's expectations—even in the early stages of the writing process—you may experience some discomfort or resistance in your efforts at getting started. Acknowledging that discomfort and talking back to it, preferably in your logbook, is one sure way of overcoming it—and also of generating even more material. The following is an example taken from a student's logbook of what can come from talking back to "the critic within," that evaluative faculty that we all possess for good reasons but which can short-circuit creativity if invoked too early:

> *I feel funny doing this so-called freewriting. It seems wrong to write this way. I was always taught to use an outline and know what you're going to say. Ms. Wilson in sixth grade was a stickler for outlines. God, everything was Roman numeralized. Numeralized?? Wonder if that's a word. Don't Numeralize me. . . . but then, the idea is to come up with things to say and write about, so how can it be wrong? It just feels funny, like running on at the mouth, out of control . . . control is so important, but should it always be?*

Notice how in talking back to the evaluative faculty, the writer above actually generates some ideas for writing about an early experience, discovers an interesting word, and acknowledges the importance of control. So long as you keep this kind of internal dialogue going on paper, the interplay between your imagination and the act of writing will continue.

Pay particular attention any time you encounter resistance while trying to do the exercises. While you may conclude that your difficulties doing an exercise are due to something you lack—for example, skill, creativity, or will—or that this book lacks, it's possible that the exercise is dredging up powerful though uncomfortable material from your subconscious—a memory, guilt, a fear—and it is at such points that you may have stunning imaginative breakthroughs.

Notice in the example above that the writer questions the importance of control. If the writer has never before acknowledged this tendency in herself, the acknowledgment here may come as a revelation and clear the way for a freer and more honest engagement with her imagination.

In our workshops, when students complain about the exercises, saying that they're difficult or weird or irrelevant, they nevertheless produce exciting results when they push themselves to complete them. In fact, those who have complained the most are among those who have turned in the most extraordinary exercises. This shouldn't surprise anyone because to complain about anything is to bring focus and strong feelings to bear on the object of complaint, two qualities of great value in the creative process. As teachers, we have come to regard moaning about the exercises as a healthy prelude to exciting discoveries.

Using a Combination of Tools

Probably no single tool that we've mentioned will be adequate to dig up or dredge up or unclog or dislodge all the imaginative material that you can bring to an exercise since each tool tends to work best with specific facets of our minds. Therefore, we encourage you to use a variety of tools and to become adroit at shifting. Begin with **freewriting,** shift to **clustering,** switch over to **brainstorming** or **listing,** look up a word on the **computer thesaurus,** and so forth, as the following student example illustrates:

I don't know what to write I don't know what to write cellophane what is cellophane it's like a cello and profanity cellophane fascinates me six wonderful things about cellophane — **FREEWRITING**

1. *it's transparent*
2. *it leaves no scars*
3. *it attracts jelly fish* — **LISTING**
4. *it tastes like chicken*
5. *it's good for keeping corpses fresh*
6. *it's better for you than iceberg lettuce*

Imagine, cellophane is used to cover iceberg lettuce and is probably better for you than the lettuce — **FOCUSED FREEWRITING**

Iceberg lettuce gets a bad rap. How to improve the reputation of iceberg lettuce

1. *Go on TV. Iceberg lettuce does a body good* — **BRAINSTORMING**
2. *Have a contest to name uses of iceberg lettuce*
3. *Have a celebrity represent iceberg lettuce*
   Who?
   a. *George Hamilton*
   b. *Heather Locklear*
   c. *Cher*
4. *Make iceberg lettuce the hero of some kind of drama*
5. *Microwave iceberg lettuce and put salt on it*
6. *Create an iceberg the size of Toledo in the shape of a head of lettuce*

But eating iceberg lettuce makes me feel empty. It's like the opposite of eating. Popcorn does the same thing to me as does watermelon . . . beginning of poem — **FOCUSED FREEWRITING**

Loving her was like dining on
iceberg lettuce: it seemed healthy <-----> *hale*
and good but it was nothing   *hearty*
less than nothing   *vigorous*
it made me hungrier.   *robust*

Loving her was like dining on
iceberg lettuce: it seemed robust
and good but it was nothing.
Less than nothing.
It made me hungrier.

Notice how the writer began with an **unfocused freewriting** that led him to the word *cellophane*. He decided to do **listing** on this discovered word and then moved to a **focused freewriting** on *iceberg lettuce,* which was a discovery from his listing activity. He **brainstormed** on iceberg lettuce, and after another brief **focused freewriting** began a poem that makes a surprising connection between iceberg lettuce and a relationship he had with a woman. While the poem is clearly just a start, it is a golden start because by giving his imagination the freedom and tools to wander, the writer has tapped into something original, fresh, and expressive.

FROM NUGGETS TO ARTIFACTS: WHAT FORM SHOULD YOU CHOOSE?

There are stories that should have been poems and essays that should have been stories. Likewise, there are those who think of themselves as story writers who show much more talent for poetry. Playwright Edward Albee, author of *Who's Afraid of Virginia Woolf,* wrote poetry for years before discovering and deciding that he was better at writing plays. A few creative writers have shown nearly equal skill and talent in more than one form of creative writing—Robert Penn Warren, poetry and fiction; Anton Chekhov, short stories and plays; Alice Walker, Joyce Carol Oates, and John Updike, fiction and poetry; Joan Didion, fiction and essays; Maya Angelou, creative nonfiction and poetry.

If you are a beginning writer, it's probably a good idea to remain open to your own potential for writing in these various forms—even if you believe you have decided to write in only one form. Likewise, it's probably a good idea to remain open to the form your beginning efforts with these exercises ultimately take.

Many excellent books have been written that define and characterize good stories, poems, and essays. As this book focuses on the ideas for generally beginning any piece of creative writing, such discussions are beyond its scope. We nevertheless include below some factors that might go into your decision to write a poem, story, or essay from the ideas generated from the exercises in this book.

Consider Writing a Poem from an Exercise If

1. The sounds of the words and the language engage you as much as the meaning.
2. The sentences develop into distinctive rhythms and patterns of repetition.
3. The images are particularly strong.
4. The sentences do not refer to a specific time or place.

Notice how the following Nugget from "Customs and the Customary" lends itself to a kind of lyric poetry, though it may well have gone in another direction:

MY HOUSE

In my house you must remove your shoes
and place them on your hands. Once
conversation begins, you may drop one
at a time to punctuate what
you are saying. In my house

you must try to draw a picture of me
and tell me why this is how you see me.
(All such efforts hang on the Great Wall, signed
and dated.) Here, no mention is ever made
of presidents, dead or living. You are expected
to rise when I rise, place a hand on my shoulder
and walk with me to the bathroom. In my house
the most venerable custom is the great dance
that takes place upon leaving: we embrace
as in a tango, re-trace our steps and conversations
and move out of the house, where I stop
turn, and you
are gone.

DOROTHY NIMS

The first line describes an ancient Asian custom, and the writer could have developed a story or even an essay about the conflicts or problems this custom has caused her. However, in the very next image of putting the shoes on the hands, the writer enters another realm, both surreal and imagistic and certainly non-literal. The repetition of "In my house" draws attention to the language and away from narrative, as do other words, like "punctuate" and the rhyme "embrace" and "re-trace." Whatever the writer's initial intentions, this piece found one form and home in poetry.

Consider Writing a Story from an Exercise If

1. The question of what happens next becomes paramount.
2. Characters and their relationships have become focal points of your exercise.
3. Scene description and dialogue emerge as significant elements.

The following Nugget from "The Briefcase" exercise has potential for both an essay about dating and single mothers or a story about what happens when one single mother tries to put off the inevitable disclosure:

> Megan hadn't meant to mislead Alan when the plastic dinosaur had fallen out of her purse. It was just that she had seen his office, with its clutter of political cartoons, his hanging rubber stork, pink slinky and other miscellaneous anti-establishment toys, and wanted him to know that she wasn't buying into the system either. So, when Alan picked it up and said "Cool" and handed the Brachiosaurus back to her with a new glimmer of recognition in his eye, she hadn't found it necessary to tell him that the toy belonged to her son, and that she had only this morning rescued it from under his car seat.
>
> Mostly she was relieved that her purse hadn't been dumped in front of him the year before when there would have been baby wipes and a spare pacifier mixed in with the usual wallet, checkbook and keys. She decided now, today, was definitely a better time.
>
> ANGELIN DONOHUE

In this passage, the careful description of character and the establishment of suspense suggest that this material might be best used in a story. We are left wondering "what happened?"—a question that is the hallmark of narrative fiction.

Consider Writing an Essay from an Exercise If

1. A lesson or moral or argument begins to emerge.
2. You want to prove or illustrate some point you touched on or discovered.
3. You want to explore the significance of an actual event.

The following beginning from the exercise "Holding On and Letting Go" feels like it is in search of some truth about human behavior:

Six A.M. I've finished shaving, bathing, talcing, fumigating, combing, shirting and slacking. All that remains is socking and, of course, shoeing. I pull open what I have come to think of as "Pandora's Drawer," not because of what might fly out of it but because of what I rarely find: two dark socks that match and that do not have holes in them. It is a fine day that meets both criteria. I have entertained the notion of throwing all these socks out and buying two dozen pairs of the same shade of black (Black, I have learned through my socks, is a Platonic ideal. Black no more exists than the tooth fairy or immortality among mortals), but throwing them all out doesn't make sense, for there are, in this drawer from hell, a few intact matching pairs. But that still doesn't explain why I don't throw out the socks with holes in them. Every morning I see coins of flesh peeking like closed eyes from these socks, but instead of throwing them out, I put them right back in the drawer where I am just as likely to do this again.

I have a Ph.D. in economics. My mother did not raise a fool. My wife did not marry one. Why can't I throw these holey socks out?

HAKI WANZO

In his exploration of his tendency to hold onto his holey socks, Haki Wanzo reflects upon how this behavior is in conflict with *his* otherwise sensible and adult behaviors. While his wife and mother are briefly mentioned, Haki is clearly the subject of the piece, a sign that an essay format is probably the right way to go here. Finally, the question he ends with—What is the significance of my action?—seems most naturally answered or tackled in an essay.

Whether you end up pursuing a specific idea from one of the exercises in a poem, story, or essay, there is no law that says you cannot go back and try it out in another form, or in all forms. The advantage you have over Michelangelo is that you are not limited to discrete slabs of marble. The material you have generated from the exercises need not be thrown away when one form doesn't work but instead can be recast into a form you are happy with.

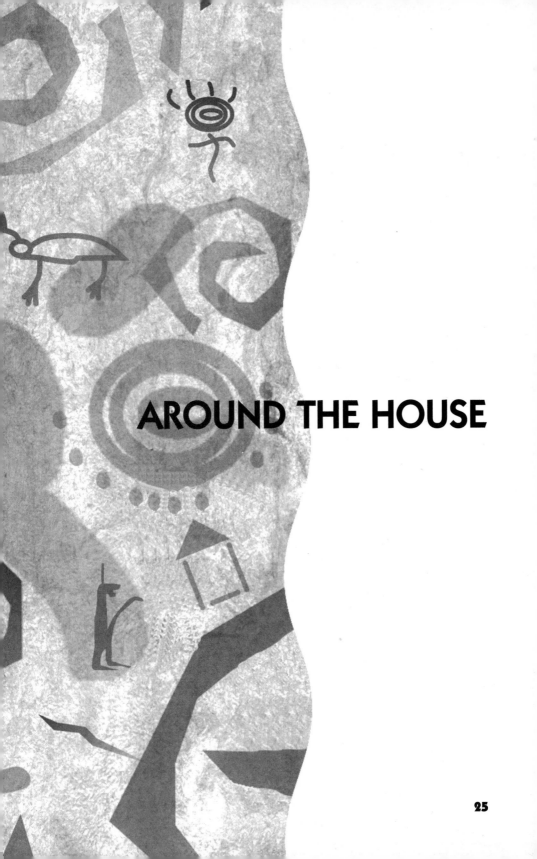

AROUND THE HOUSE

WHY I WILL NOT GET OUT OF BED

Most of us have days when the world outside our bedroom seems too difficult to face. We skip school, call in sick, put off our errands until tomorrow, and spend the rest of the day feeling at once guilty and relieved as life generally goes on quite well without us.

Many view the decision to spend the day in bed as a passive choice, something we give in to when we lack the necessary physical or emotional energy to do much else. But it takes energy *not* to function in the way that is expected of us, to take a day off from the rhythm of our lives and spend time alone with only our inner resources for company. This exercise asks you to explore the reasons for making such a choice, to examine the forces that make you wish you could stay in bed certain mornings.

PANNING INSTRUCTIONS

1.   Brainstorm all the reasons you can think of for *not* getting out of bed. What is it about your day that you don't want to face? Get into your most negative frame of mind to imagine every possible thing that is wrong and might go wrong out there.

2.   Start a poem, story, or essay in which you justify your decision to stay in bed by including as many of the reasons you have come up with as possible.

EXCAVATING INSTRUCTIONS

Sometimes we have trouble getting out of bed not because we're avoiding what is waiting for us but because we're avoiding what is *not* waiting for us.

We may have trouble getting out of bed when someone we care about has moved away or died or when an emotion we have come to count on to make our life feel complete has faded. Getting out of bed then becomes a metaphor for facing a loss that we may not be ready to confront.

Begin a poem, story, or essay in which you explore an emotional reason for not getting out of bed. Robert Jackson, for example, is slowed down by the news of his death (see below). Notice the way James Tate builds to his revelation in "Why I Will Not Get Out of Bed" (page 29), but ultimately saves the revelation for the final lines.

 **NUGGETS**

FROM THE BEGINNING OF AN ESSAY

The first thing I heard this morning when the clock radio went off was the news that I had been put to death in the gas chamber in Tallahassee, Florida.

This news was being reported because the man with my name—an admittedly common name—had spent a record number of years on death row, something like thirty-five years or maybe forty years, I don't know. The point is, what I heard when that radio went off was "Robert Jackson was put to death this morning at 5:03 A.M."

My wife heard it too, and her first reaction was to say, "Good, guess you don't have to go to work." But it wasn't my first reaction, though I didn't in fact want to get out of bed. It set me back, hearing this. It made me want to pull the covers over my head and just spend the day thinking about my life

ROBERT JACKSON

■

WHY I WILL NOT GET OUT OF BED

I can't go down the hall
To see if she's survived
Another night,
To see if her will is stronger
Than her cells.
The battle of the white and red
Rages.

There is no neutrality
Where there are feelings.
Yet on the battle grounds
I cannot fight for her,
Only watch
Each time she falters.
Uncover my soul and see
If there is a smile I can offer.
I have no bravery.
Multiply, divide, and conquer.
I cannot bear who wins.

PATTY SEATON

WHY I WILL NOT GET OUT OF BED

The sheets are holding me
prisoner: clever grabbers,
breath-stealers.
They think they're very funny
indeed.

If I put my foot out
the rug snarls and
seizes my ankles.
I'll be tossed
high into the hallway,
thrown in a heap at
the bottom of the stairs.

Mostly I hate the way
the kitchen smirks
and unhinges its jaws:
how it gorges on my sleep,
how it gags on my dreams.

LIZ ENAGONIO

 **ARTIFACTS**

WHY I WILL NOT GET OUT OF BED

My muscles unravel
like spools of ribbon:
there is not a shadow

of pain. I will pose
like this for the rest
of the afternoon,

for the remainder
of all noons. The rain
is making a valley

of my dim features.
I am in Albania,
I am on the Rhine.

It is autumn,
I smell the rain,
I see children running

through columbine.
I am honey,
I am several winds.

My nerves dissolve,
my limbs wither—
I don't love you.

I don't love you.

JAMES TATE

HOLDING ON AND LETTING GO

Many of us have difficulty letting go of things that have lost their usefulness. Clothes that never fit take up a third of our closets; date books and desk calendars optimistically purchased to help us organize our days wait to be scribbled in; the rowing machine bought with the healthiest of intentions stands up in the back of the closet like a skeleton. We hold on to much of this stuff because throwing it out would be to acknowledge defeat or, worse, change.

Sometimes we've outgrown an old life where barbells or crocheting needles made sense; sometimes that life never really fit us right in the first place. Hidden away for years, these dust collectors only go public when we sell them through the classifieds, donate them to charity, or turn them out on the lawn for a yard sale.

In places where others find dustballs and fire hazards, a writer can discover gold. The following exercises are designed to help you spin gold out of some of your forgotten "collections."

PANNING INSTRUCTIONS

1. Discover what you have difficulty letting go of by rummaging through your drawers, closets, refrigerator, and, of course, under the bed. If you have them, attics, garages, and basements can also be excellent discovery places as long as you don't become overwhelmed or, worse, start cleaning.

Anything you do not use or have not used for a long time counts. For example, one person may discover a cache of plastic L'eggs pantyhose "eggs" in the back of her drawer while another person may find eight different brands of salsa in the refrigerator, some dating back to the Carter administration and home to green and purple colonies of fungi.

Brainstorm uses for any of your uncovered treasures. Try to come up with at least five uses, as in the example below:

What My Seventeen Pantyhose Eggs Are Good For:

- Filling with stones and shaking to music

- Filling with water and throwing from my window at people who irritate me

- Hiding under a sleeping chicken to see what she does when she wakes up

- Sending as Easter gifts if I sent Easter gifts

- Rolling down the stairs all at once to see which one is fastest

2. **Freewrite** on reasons why it is so hard to throw out or get rid of things that are no longer truly useful. Begin a poem, story, or essay that explores this difficulty, as Haki Wanzo does in his essay "Dark Holes" (see below).

EXCAVATING INSTRUCTIONS

Often things we are reluctant to throw out bring up memories of old relationships, places we have lived, or other lives we have led. For example, consider Mrs. Havisham's wedding dress in Charles Dickens' *Great Expectations* (see page 32). An accidental ashtray collection discovered under a kitchen sink might remind someone of the pain of quitting smoking or the life he had when he still smoked. Several well-worn pairs of size five, black jeans might remind someone else of her life before she became pregnant with her first child.

Work on a story, poem, or personal essay that explores the emotions elicited by the things you discovered for the panning exercise.

NUGGETS

FROM THE ESSAY "DARK HOLES"

Six A.M. I've finished shaving, bathing, talcing, fumigating, combing, shirting and slacking. All that remains is socking and, of course, shoeing. I pull open what I have come to think of as "Pandora's Drawer," not because of what might fly out of it but because of what I rarely find: two dark socks that match and that do not have holes in them. It is a fine day that meets both criteria. I have entertained the notion of throwing all these socks out and buying two dozen pairs of the same shade of black (Black, I have learned through my socks, is a Platonic ideal. Black no more exists than the tooth fairy or immortality among mortals), but throwing them all out doesn't make sense, for there are, in this drawer from hell, a few intact matching pairs. But that still doesn't explain why I don't throw out the socks with holes in them. Every morning I see coins of flesh peeking like closed eyes from these socks, but instead of throwing them out, I put them right back in the drawer where I am just as likely to do this again.

I have a Ph.D. in economics.

My mother did not raise a fool.

My wife did not marry one.

Why can't I throw these holey socks out?

HAKI WANZO

 **ARTIFACTS**

FROM THE NOVEL *GREAT EXPECTATIONS*

She was dressed in rich materials—satins, and lace, and silks—all of white. . . . She had not quite finished dressing, for she had but one shoe on—the other was on the table near her hand—her veil was but half arranged, her watch and chain were not put on, and some lace for her bosom lay with those trinkets, and with her handkerchief, and gloves, and some flowers, and a prayer book, all confusedly heaped about the looking glass.

. . . But, I saw that everything within my view which ought to be white, had been white long ago, and had lost its lustre, and was faded and yellow. I saw that the bride within the bridal dress had withered like the dress, and like the flowers, and had no brightness left but the brightness of her sunken eyes.

CHARLES DICKENS

■

YARD SALE

Nothing has prepared us for the man
who knows the current world
market value of cut glass bowls
or the connoisseur of broken speakers.

We are shy and flattered they want
our things and amazed at the things
they want: a chipped drinking glass
with a frieze of pink babies, a chair
as dark and thin as Don Quixote.

Even the purple and blue cubist painting
that looked like the ragged birth of some animal
sells—and at a price much higher
than we imagined. "Say what you will
about realism," the buyer says, "color
is always in." But how to price

bone white cylinders with deckled lids
when we don't even know what they are,
how they work, where, in our lives,
they come from. And we wonder now
if we're letting go of something
valuable or important or just
lucky and mysterious, like tonsils.
Perhaps the life turned out
on the lawn is the one we should live—
the life within, the one we should sell.

A woman with a baby carriage full
of spatulas backs carefully down
our driveway. Say what we will
about realism, it's not a question
of how many more eggs she can turn.

MICHAEL C. SMITH

PARTY INVITATIONS

When was the last time you had a party? As we get older, we may let our birthdays slip by, sometimes hoping they won't be noticed, but holidays like New Year's Eve and the Fourth of July often remain cause for celebration. For many, parties mark transitions—Memorial Day picnics welcome the beginning of summer, while Labor Day picnics symbolize the close of the season. Bar mitzvahs, baby showers, weddings, and retirement parties all herald the future as they say goodbye to the past.

Still, important landmarks in our lives often go unnoted. Who was there to congratulate you when you made the last payment on a four-year car note? Who patted you on the back when you finally figured out how to program your VCR? Where were the flowers and cards when your three-year-old realized you could do something else with a potty besides filling it with blocks? What makes one event worthy of commemoration and another unworthy? The following exercise asks you to pay tribute to your own overlooked life markers by throwing a party in their honor.

PLANNING INSTRUCTIONS

1. What important events in your own life have you let slip by without a celebration? Make a **list** of all that come to mind. Mix in the grand with the mundane, as in the sample list below:

- Taking my first airplane trip
- Finding the perfect winter coat
- Getting divorced
- Learning how to make hollandaise sauce
- Paying off my student loan

34

2. Choose an item from your list and create an invitation to a party in its celebration. What is the right kind of party for this event? Fill in the following blanks on your invitation in ways that befit the seriousness or silliness of the occasion:

Occasion: Divorce Party

Date: June 22, the first anniversary of my divorce—full moon expected.

Time: Two A.M., the time of night I still sometimes miss my ex-spouse despite everything.

Place: The kitchen, where we'll re-enact the famous plate-throwing scene that marked the last week of the relationship.

Bring: No single men—I am tired of being set up. Shoulder to cry on optional.

Wear: A devious smile—the last laugh will be on him.

Rain Date: One year later.

3. Using the details you have just gathered, try beginning an invitation poem, story, or essay. Approach your poem or story as if this event is truly forthcoming. In your essay, explore the reasons why you wish you could throw such a celebration, as Andrew Lawson does in his essay "I Celebrate Myself—Sort Of" (see below).

EXCAVATING INSTRUCTIONS

Write an extended invitation to participate in an abstract, psychological, or spiritual event. Imagine throwing a party to celebrate the color purple, the shape of a triangle, the end of a depression, or a religious revelation. What is the real subject of James Tate's poem "The Coming Out of Ourselves Party" (page 36)?

NUGGETS

FROM THE ESSAY "I CELEBRATE MYSELF—SORT OF"

I'm not a big partier. In fact, I don't even celebrate my own birthday— nor do I allow others to do so. There was one occasion though that I really wanted to do up in a big way, even though my friends said I was nuts and no one BUT NO ONE understood.

To understand why I would want to celebrate this occasion, which I'll tell you right now was the day my braces came off, you would need to know that having straight teeth was the only obsession my parents shared and that, ultimately, it wasn't enough to hold them together. My braces, in fact, outlasted their marriage: the divorce decree provided for their removal and stipulated that my father would pay for the procedure, which took only about ten minutes. . . . I wanted to celebrate their removal because my braces in dozens of ways complicated the way I thought about my parents, love, sex, adolescence, and the meaning of life.

ANDREW LAWSON

 **ARTIFACTS**

THE COMING OUT OF OURSELVES PARTY

You wanted to be strong.
I wanted to congratulate all of us
on giving in.
Gum wrappers are wriggling in the sun.
Mrs. Mendosa's voice rattles
around Jefferson Street two times,
and ends spinning
like a BB in a can.

Then I thought of all the women
I had ever had. I appreciate
the patronage; thanks for dropping in.
But the King relinquishes his zither.

We were last together
at the Colonial Inn, in Concord, Massachusetts.
We had a free television;
sixty air-conditioned rooms,
including the Thoreau Room,
The Emerson Bar and The Hawthorne John.
You wanted to have integrity.
What a day, the clerk said.

The sky is disheveling overhead.
The pulse of the earth is slowing.
On this street there is not even a radio.
The days continue to eat each other;

the doors grow little and thick.
Always, finally, we are untouched.

This was to be the coming out of ourselves party,
to which we all looked forward.
This was to be bigger than life;
this, the inside story.

JAMES TATE

BAGGAGE

For every person who brags about spending a summer traveling around the country with nothing but a small backpack containing three pairs of socks and a camera, there is another person who packs an entire wardrobe for a two-week stay at a nearby beach. When we pack, we are forced to confront our essential natures. The classic worrier hides traveler's checks in three separate bags and memorizes his credit card numbers in case they are stolen. The workaholic packs an extra battery pack for her notebook computer. And the serious sightseer brings three different travel guides.

Still, we make mistakes, anticipating formal dinners only to wind up eating fast food. We forget that drugstores exist in other cities, and even other countries, and we scoop up handfuls of trial size bottles of shampoo and shaving cream and line our suitcases with them, only to take half of them back home again.

And no matter how well we think we've packed, most of us have had the experience of forgetting something as basic as a toothbrush or as important as the first page of a report for a business presentation.

PLANNING INSTRUCTIONS

1. Make a **list** of several items you have forgotten to pack for a vacation or business trip. Notice Joan Didion's "significant omission" in the excerpt from her essay "The White Album" (page 40).

2. Make a second list of items you have packed but *didn't* need or use once you got to your destination.

3. Make a third list of unlikely things to either pack or forget to pack for a trip. For example, a list might begin the following way:

- A pink flamingo

- My first-grade report card

- A towel Mick Jagger wiped his forehead with

4.   To help you begin to get started on a story, poem, or piece of creative nonfiction that takes off from these lists, try completing some of the following statements with truths, lies, or a combination of the two:

- I opened my bag and was horrified that I had forgotten to pack _____ .

- The _____ I packed proved totally useless.

- I never thought that _____ would come in handy, but it sure did.

- When I opened my suitcase, I was surprised to find I had packed _____ .

- My _____ (mother, husband, sister, etc.) told me not to bring my _____, but of course I didn't listen.

EXCAVATING INSTRUCTIONS

Psychologists claim we all carry psychic "baggage" around with us—wounds from our childhoods, betrayals by ex-lovers. Make a list of some of the baggage you carry. For example, someone's list might begin the following way:

- Anger from that time my father grounded me for two weeks when I got caught shoplifting.
- Sadness from my miscarriage.

Pack the story, poem, or essay that you began in Panning in one of these pieces of "baggage" by bringing that emotion to your writing. One way of doing this is to have the items you have either forgotten or remembered become metaphors for an enduring feeling. For an example of this, notice the way the character in the excerpt from Jud McClosky's short story (page 40) packs electrical extension cords—perhaps because of his insecurity over losing touch with power.

NUGGETS

FROM THE SHORT STORY "THE KING'S GOPHER"

After tipping the bellhop, he turned to the task of unpacking the suitcase he had so meticulously packed nearly a week ago. The socks were rolled in little balls and lay nestled in the corner of the suitcase like dark eggs. There were the usual slacks, shirts and underwear, but there were also three electrical extension cords lined up in the satin pockets around the sides of the suitcase. From his many years of travel he had learned that there are never enough outlets in hotels, even though he rarely if ever needed to plug something in. He placed the extension cords in the same drawer with his belts.

He unpacked quickly because he was anxious to call the regional office to find out if Howard Winston, the vice president of marketing, had arrived. They weren't scheduled to meet until late the next day, but he liked to know where Winston was at all times. Even in New York, he would sometimes call Winston's secretary just to learn what he already knew, that he was tied up in some meeting or other. More than a hobby, tracking the executives was the only way he knew of getting a handle on his fear that he was losing touch with the power in the organization. It gave him a sense of control, and sometimes it gave him just enough information to allow him a night's sleep.

JUD McCLOSKY

ARTIFACTS

FROM THE ESSAY "THE WHITE ALBUM"

To Pack and Wear:

> *2 skirts*
> *2 jerseys or leotards*
> *1 pullover sweater*
> *2 pair shoes*
> *stockings*
> *bra*
> *nightgown, robe, slippers*
> *cigarettes*

bourbon
bag with:
   shampoo
   toothbrush and paste
   Basis soap
   razor, deodorant
   aspirin, prescriptions, Tampax
   face cream, powder, baby oil
To Carry:
   mohair throw
   typewriter
   2 legal pads and pens
   files
   house key

This is a list which was taped inside my closet door in Hollywood during those years when I was reporting more or less steadily. The list enabled me to pack, without thinking, for any piece I was likely to do. Notice the deliberate anonymity of costume: in a skirt, a leotard, *and stockings,* I could pass on either side of the culture. Notice the mohair throw for trunk-line flights (i.e., no blankets) and for the motel room in which the air conditioning could not be turned off. Notice the bourbon for the same motel room. Notice the typewriter for the airport, coming home: the idea was to turn in the Hertz car, check in, find an empty bench, and start typing the day's notes.

It should be clear that this was a list made by someone who prized control, yearned after momentum, someone determined to play her role as if she had the script, heard her cues, knew the narrative. There is on this list one significant omission, one article I needed and never had: a watch. I needed a watch not during the day, when I could turn on the car radio or ask someone, but at night, in the motel. Quite often I would ask the desk for the time every half hour or so, until finally, embarrassed to ask again, I would call Los Angeles and ask my husband. In other words I had skirts, jerseys, leotards, pullover sweater, shoes, stockings, bra, nightgown, robe, slippers, cigarettes, bourbon, shampoo, toothbrush and paste, Basis soap, razor, deodorant, aspirin, prescriptions, Tampax, face cream, powder, baby oil, mohair throw, typewriter, legal pads, pens, files and a house key, but I didn't know what time it was. This may be a parable, either of my life as a reporter during this period or of the period itself.

JOAN DIDION

From the story "The Things They Carried"

The things they carried were largely determined by necessity. Among the necessities or near necessities were P-38 can openers, pocket knives, heat tabs, wrist watches, dog tags, mosquito repellent, chewing gum, candy, salt tablets, packets of Kool Aid, lighters, matches, sewing kits, Military Payment Certificates, C rations, and two or three canteens of water. . . . On their feet they carried jungle boots—2.1 pounds—and Dave Jensen carried three pairs of socks and a can of Dr. Scholl's foot powder as a precaution against trench foot. Until he was shot, Ted Lavender carried six or seven ounces of premium dope, which for him was a necessity. Mitchell Sanders, the RTO[2], carried condoms. Norman Bowker carried a diary. Rat Kiley carried comic books. Kiowa, a devout Baptist, carried an illustrated New Testament that had been presented to him by his father, who taught Sunday school in Oklahoma City, Oklahoma. As a hedge against bad times, however, Kiowa also carried his grandmother's distrust of the white man, his grandfather's old hunting hatchet. Necessity dictated.

Tim O'Brien

AT THE DINNER TABLE

ociologists lament the fact that few of us sit down with our families each night to eat dinner together anymore. Instead, we catch the end of the evening news on television or chat on the phone with a friend while stuffing down a slice of cold pizza. While modern life may seem overly hectic and leave us longing for lost traditions, in truth many of us are privately relieved to give up the daily ritual of the family meal.

Family meals are inherently emotionally charged, even in the most reserved families. Stepsisters, who were fighting over the phone only minutes before, are forced to sit next to each other and pass the peas. Working parents hurry and try to catch up on their children's days even as their children are rolling their eyes and asking to be excused. Often our expectations—whether we long for harmony, serious conversation, or simply a feeling of togetherness—are dashed as the meatloaf dries out on the counter and the second glass of milk spills and fans out across the table. Still, it is there amid the chaos, disappointments, and second helpings of three-alarm chili that many of our memories remain.

PANNING INSTRUCTIONS

1. Think back to your childhood dinner, lunch, or breakfast table. (Some of us will have to think back further than others.) Even if you only ate as a family one or two meals a week (or month), focus on those meals. **Freewrite** for ten minutes on your family meals. If you find yourself getting stuck, prompt yourself by focusing on the smells and tastes of the foods you ate together.

2. Draw a simple sketch of your family's table. Was it round? Square? Oblong? Where did everyone sit? Draw pictures of your family members (you don't have to be an artist; stick figures will do) and seat them in their appropriate places at the table. Note the conflicts that existed between family members by writing applicable notes near the drawing that represents them (for example,

"Mary resents Tony because he was the first to take her place as the only child—will never sit next to him.").

3.   What were some of the typical meals you ate? **List** several as you remember them and briefly note your reactions to them, as in the list below:

MEAL	REACTION
• Macaroni and cheese	Felt loved when my mother remembered to sprinkle bread crumbs on top the way I liked.
• TV dinners	Fought with my brother over who got the one that had the brownie for dessert.
• Bacon and eggs	My father cooked these on Sundays sometimes before the divorce. Bacon often burned but tasted good anyway.

4.   Begin a poem, short story, or personal essay in which you bring to life a particular meal at your childhood table. Choose a meal that is both ordinary *and* memorable. Perhaps an announcement of some kind was made (maybe someone was fired from a job, made cheerleading squad, was expelled from school, had joined a convent, or was moving to Mexico) or a family member had either joined the table (through birth, adoption, remarriage, and so on) or left (through divorce, death, high school graduation, and so forth).

Comb through your prewriting, and choose the most *telling* concrete details—those that appeal to our sense of smell, taste, touch, hearing, and sight. If you're writing poem or story, feel free to create characters and events. Try to incorporate stressful interactions that might have taken place. In the excerpt from the novel *Dinner at the Homesick Restaurant* (page 45), notice the tension between the three children and their mother, Pearl, soon after Pearl's husband has left them. In the short story "A Family Supper," notice that much of the tension exists in what is left *unsaid*. And in the excerpt from Madelyn Callahan (page 45), notice that the dinner table serves as a unifying context for describing characters and their relationships.

EXCAVATING INSTRUCTIONS

Take a step away from the table and try looking at yourself from the perspective of another family member. Write a piece in which a sibling, parent, or other relative tells a dinner table story that focuses on your behavior and features a major event in your life.

Or bring together in a story, essay, or poem controversial figures from your life (enemies, old bosses, teachers, and so on) both past and present. Consider also including a few celebrities (Kevin Costner, for example). At this spectacularly odd dinner, introduce one topic for everyone to discuss and record the imaginary dialogue and interactions.

NUGGETS

FROM THE ESSAY "AT THE DINNER TABLE"

My father sat at the head of a large rectangular table, which overwhelmed the living and dining space in our Rob-and-Laura-Petrie-style home. At the other end of the table, my maternal grandmother made her nightly disapprovals clear with her stony silences and her expressionless mouth. To my father's right, my mother juggled dishes and serving utensils furiously, because, as I recall, the woman was consistently furious day and night. Between my parents was wedged the small, fat protoplasm with lungs that became my brother. . . .

I always sat at my father's left, torturing my older sister who was perfect. Perfectly neat. Perfectly attired. Perfectly coifed. Far more savvy than even Madonna, she created a myth of her own perfection at the age of seven.

MADELYN CALLAHAN

ARTIFACTS

FROM THE NOVEL *DINNER AT THE HOMESICK RESTAURANT*

The sounds from the kitchen were different now—cutlery rattling, glassware clinking. Their mother must be setting the table. Pretty soon she'd serve supper. Cody had such a loaded feeling in his throat, he never wanted to eat again. . . .

They filed down, dragging their feet. They stopped at the first-floor bathroom and meticulously scrubbed their hands, taking extra pains with the backs. Each one waited for the others. Then they went into the kitchen. Their mother was slicing a brick of Spam. She didn't look at them, but she started speaking the instant they were seated. "It's not enough that I should have to work till 5:00 P.M., no; then I come home and find nothing seen to, no chores done, you children off till all hours with disreputable characters in the alleys or wasting your time with school chorus, club meetings. . . ."

She sat serenely, as if finished with the subject forever, and reached for a bowl of peas. Jenny's face was streaming with tears, but she wasn't making a sound and Pearl seemed unaware of her. Cody cleared his throat. . . .

The three of them washed the dishes, dried them, and put them away in the cupboards. They wiped the table and countertops and swept the kitchen floor. The sight of any crumb or stain was a relief, a pleasure; they attacked it with Bon Ami.

ANNE TYLER

■

FROM THE SHORT STORY "A FAMILY SUPPER"

Supper was waiting in a dimly lit room next to the kitchen. The only source of light was a big lantern that hung over the table, casting the rest of the room in shadow. We bowed to each other before starting the meal.

There was little conversation. When I made some polite comment about the food, Kikuko giggled a little. Her earlier nervousness seemed to have returned to her. My father did not speak for several minutes. Finally he said:

"It must feel strange for you, being back in Japan."

"Yes, it is a little strange."

"Already, perhaps, you regret leaving America."

"A little. Not so much. I didn't leave behind much. Just some empty rooms."

"I see."

I glanced across the table. My father's face looked stony and forbidding in the half-light. We ate on in silence.

KAZUO ISHIGURO

PAPER TRAILS

Those who have gone through the agony of an IRS audit know the value of canceled checks and credit-card receipts as records of possible deductible expenses. But these documents are more than that. Pull out a stack of canceled checks or credit-card statements from several years ago and go through them. Notice how your life, or your spending, has changed over the years. If you're like most people, the majority of the checks will be for payment of routine bills: the rent, utilities, credit-card payments, car payments, and so on. But even these common expenses change (usually for the worse). Mixed in with the routine checks you'll also find one-time payments that often reflect significant events during certain periods of your life. For example, the $5 check paid to the county for a marriage license (remember your consternation at not having cash); the $1,700 you paid out-of-pocket for necessary dental work (at the time, and even now, an extraordinary amount of money); the $30 check for an office visit to the doctor and an examination that confirmed a pregnancy. Among the canceled checks and credit-card statements may be large purchases you have no memory of, and smaller checks—the $2.50 fee to enter a park—that you strangely remember. The longer you do this, the more these documents become records of milestones in your life.

The following exercises ask you to exploit your canceled checks and credit-card statements as personal resources for your writing. For this exercise, you obviously need to have had a checking account and/or credit cards and, ideally, access to at least three years' worth of statements or receipts.

PANNING INSTRUCTIONS

Look over a group of canceled checks and credit-card statements, and make a **list** of items for which you paid about the same amount of money. For example, you may have written three checks for $25 each—one check to a baby-sitter, another to purchase a camping tent, and another for a pair of jeans.

Try to connect several checks written for a similar amount in a poem, story, or essay.

EXCAVATING INSTRUCTIONS

1. From your collection of canceled checks and credit-card statements, choose five or six purchases made around the same time that evoke strong feelings or memories or that seem particularly revealing. Notice how humorist Art Buchwald, in "Credit Card" (see page 49), uses the occasion of the theft of one of his credit cards to reveal his tastes. Begin a poem, story, or essay about what was going on in your life when these checks were written. The piece should integrate the information on all the checks.

For example, the student poem "The Giraffe" (see below) uses the following information from checks the student wrote in 1979:

#506, July 16, Toys-R-Us	$178.00
#507, July 19, John Elman, Atty	$3,290.00
#508, August 10, IRS	$2,140.19
#509, August 12, Towson Funeral Services	$7,200.00

2. Or from both canceled checks and credit-card statements, take note of those expenses that arose in an emergency of some sort, and use these incidents in a poem, story, or essay.

 **NUGGETS**

THE GIRAFFE

I bought a giraffe the size of a house
for my grandson just before my wife died.
It wasn't an easy time, but the giraffe
struck me funny, so much so
that when the IRS and my attorney
came knocking, I let them in
to my savings. What matter? My grandson
doesn't know what to do with the giraffe,
but he shows it off and his friends come over
and they all stare up at it. I've never seen a toy

that big. I've never seen anything
that big.

Arnold Petrowski

# **ARTIFACTS**

From the column "Credit Card"

Recently one of my credit cards was stolen. The problem was that I was unaware of the theft, and therefore the criminal had use of the card for thirty days. . . .

"Did you have fun in Puerto Rico?" my accountant wanted to know.

"Not really," I told him. "Mainly because I haven't been there in ten years."

"Well, you got a credit card bill for three thousand dollars for a stay there, and it looks as if you had a wonderful shopping spree. I wish you would tell your wife to buy quarts instead of gallons of Joy perfume."

"That wasn't my wife," I protested. "She hates Joy. It's obvious that someone else is using my card. . . ."

"You don't have to pay the charges once you report the loss," he assured me.

"I'm not worried about that. I'm concerned he's going to hurt my reputation as a big spender. Suppose he buys his socks at People's Drug Store? . . ."

". . . Your friend bought a beautiful cashmere jacket at Barney's for fourteen hundred dollars."

"Single- or double-breasted?"

"Single."

"That's good," I said. "I hate double-breasted."

Art Buchwald

DANCING WITH DAD

J ust as we sing brilliantly in the shower, many of us dance brilliantly when we are alone and in the privacy of our living rooms and often when we are cleaning and dusting or doing dishes, our partners a princely broom or a vampish bath towel. We dance the way we danced as children when it was possible for any of us to grow up and become a chorus line dancer, a vaudeville star, or even a prima ballerina. Which is to say brilliantly.

As writers we dance with language. Prose and poetry, like all dance types and forms, involve meaning, movement, and rhythm. It's not surprising to find words associated with dance used to describe qualities in writing, to hear expressions like "The words flow gracefully over the page." "The stanzas lumbered clumsily." "Her images leapt off the page."

In the following exercises, try your hand at creating dances in prose or poetry and discovering in the process the kind of dancer you already are.

PANNING INSTRUCTIONS

1. **List** the names of as many dance types and forms as you can think of in ten minutes. One person's list might begin as follows: ballet, jazz dance, clogging, line dancing, ballroom, the waltz, the tango, the jitterbug, the Charleston, the electric slide, and the lambada.

2. For each item on the list, **freewrite** your impressions and observations of the dance and its name. (If you've only heard the name of a dance but have never seen it performed, simply jot down your impressions of the name of the dance and anything you've heard about it.) In your freewrites, try to address kinds of movement, rhythm, and meanings associated with each form or type of dance.

3. Choose one or two dance forms or types that inspired you to generate a lot of freewriting, and start a poem, story, or essay that in some way corresponds to your descriptions and relationship to the dance, or, alternatively, consider an ironic treatment such as that in Theodore Roethke's famous poem "My Papa's Waltz" (page 52). Do the movements described correspond to a waltz?

You may choose to write about yourself alone (dancing with that dish rag) or in a relationship with someone else. For example, say that with the word "tango," someone's freewrite featured the following descriptions: "strong, definitive, bold, turning, a little unpredictable, passionate." Now he might want to write about a relationship he had when he behaved this way or wished he had behaved this way:

> *Her eyes were dark and wide*
> *I saw her smile*
> *And I asked her why*
> *She wouldn't say*
> *So I took her hand*
> *and made her rise*
> *and we danced all night. . . .*

EXCAVATING INSTRUCTIONS

As children we all danced with our parents, even if music was never played in our houses. When a three-year-old reaches into a cookie jar and says "Just *one* more" to a mother he knows will bend, he is dancing with her. When a teenager asks her father for permission to stay out until midnight after her mother has denied it, she is dancing. Figurative family dances consist of familiar movements that create generally predictable outcomes.

Focus on a figurative dance you engaged in with family members, and make it literal by turning it into an actual dance. For example, a writer who finds herself dancing with her stepdaughter around the topic of her dropping out of school might begin her piece this way: "In the kitchen we twirl past each other, our hands covering our eyes. We peek through our fingers at each other as we twirl again, pretending not to notice that the other one can see." In "Classical Family" (page 52), Helen Schwartz embraces all the members of her family in almost courtly fashion.

Begin in motion, use the present tense, and just take off, describing steps and moves and rhythms, the particulars of place, the attitudes and gestures, allowing yourself to digress and return. If you find yourself drifting into a poem, story, or some point you would like to make in an essay, pursue your inclination.

NUGGETS

CLASSICAL FAMILY

My brother, my parents and I
have been fighting for days.
We argue over what to do
what to eat, what to see
what to think. We invite
and dismiss dozens of issues
and topics and we do so
in such a regular and rhythmic
way that soon we rise, line up
and glide in and out of a minuet
though I'm not sure what it is.
All I know is that we are stately
as we move through the center of ourselves
and out the other side on issues,
my father bowing, my mother curtsying
my brother huffy like a young lord.
It is classical what we do.
We are a classical family.

HELEN SCHWARTZ

ARTIFACTS

MY PAPA'S WALTZ

The whiskey on your breath
Could make a small boy dizzy;
But I hung on like death:
Such waltzing was not easy.

We romped until the pans
Slid from the kitchen shelf;
My mother's countenance
Could not unfrown itself.

The hand that held my wrist
Was battered on one knuckle;

At every step you missed
My right ear scraped your buckle.

You beat time on my head
With a palm caked hard by dirt,
Then waltzed me off to bed
Still clinging to your shirt

Theodore Roethke

THE SPICE RACK

Variety is indeed the spice of life, and most of us have on hand a variety of spices, strong and subtle, liquid and dry, to testify to that truth. In all cultures throughout history, spices have been valued nearly as much as gold. Trade in exotic spices prompted Columbus and other explorers and merchants to take to the high seas to discover new routes as well as new spices, and the quest for more spice has prompted many people to go to extraordinary lengths.

Along with their enchanting odors and tastes, the names of spices also conjure up the exotic—tarragon, paprika, oregano, turmeric, coriander, cream of tartar, rosemary, basil, saffron, cumin, cayenne, curry.

The following exercises ask you to add spice to your writing by inventing characters with the names of spices and then developing these characters with behaviors that in some ways match the spice of their namesake.

PANNING INSTRUCTIONS

1. **List** the names of the spices you have in your kitchen. Skip a few lines to give yourself room to write about each one.

2. Beside each name, describe the physical qualities of the spice: its odor, color, texture, taste. Also briefly record your reaction to and impressions of the spice—for example, "too hot for me; I'd use it sparingly if at all. Reminds me of India even though it's not a spice found in East Indian food."

3. Choose a couple of spices whose names or qualities interest you, and for each create a person's name—for example, Mrs. Curry, General Tarragon, John Salt.

4. Describe your characters using the notes you made about the spices. Be very liberal with your descriptions, and let yourself take off on scenes if they begin to emerge, as Angelin Donohue does with her character Cinnamon Brown (see below).

If you are working on an essay instead of a fictional piece or poem, decide which real characters in your life already fit the characteristics of certain spices. (For example, perhaps your boss reminds you of salt because the only way you can take him is with a grain of salt. Your niece seems a lot like cumin—earthy and a little exotic.)

EXCAVATING INSTRUCTIONS

Most of us are familiar with variations of the expression "It adds spice to my life." The "it" could be anything from a class in harmonica to an extramarital affair. The question is, what is the nature of the spice that has been added?

For this exercise, choose an activity from your life or someone else's life that would qualify as "adding spice" and relate this activity to an actual spice in a poem, essay, or fictional scene. Notice how Karen Weiss uses the attributes of pepper to describe tennis lessons in her short story (page 56).

NUGGETS

FROM A SHORT STORY IN PROGRESS

When people met Cinnamon Brown, the first thing they noticed was that she didn't quite live up to her name. It wasn't just that her coloring was on the pale side. It was that she lacked the implicit sweetness and zest of the spice. Cinnamon had taken to wearing beige, only the palest beige, which seemed to be almost a skin tone. She often looked as if she wasn't wearing anything at all. In spite of her benign appearance, she was openly disdainful of people her own age who liked animals, and anyone her parents' age who dared to use a superlative. So when her cousins came to visit and claimed they wanted to see her city's wonderful zoo, they were met with a glassy stare that disavowed all acknowledgment of them.

Her sister, Ginger, was really more to everyone's liking. They said she was spunky, upbeat, and funny in an odd way. The neighbors attributed her sense of humor to her ability to adjust to being the youngest sister in the family. Although she never asked, Ginger often wondered what her parents had been thinking when they had named her and pondered the possibility of other hapless siblings called Clove and Nutmeg.

ANGELIN DONOHUE

■

FROM THE STORY "UP CLOSE TO THE NET AND PERSONAL"

I've been taking tennis lessons for two years now. What do I know? I know follow through. For two years I've been looking across the net at this guy named Skip who's telling me to bend when I hit a ball when my body longs to bend down and take a nap. Still, I can't help notice that Skip is a good looking young man, probably too young for me, probably more appropriate for my niece. But she's at Columbia and Skip is where he should be: selling tennis lessons and handing out white towels.

I'm not a good player, never will be, despite Skip's smiling encouragement. The tennis lessons are like what I put on food to make me think I'm eating better than I am. Like freshly grated pepper. It upgrades my fried potatoes, irritates my eyes a little sometimes, but it doesn't cost too much. And my life, God knows, is like fried potatoes. Did I say that?

KAREN WEISS

ARTIFACTS

ROSEMARY

Beauty and Beauty's son and rosemary—
Venus and Love, her son, to speak plainly—
born of the sea supposedly,
braids a garland of festivity,
     Not always rosemary

since the flight to Egypt, blooming differently.
With lancelike leaf, green but silver underneath,
its flowers—white originally—
turned blue. The herb of memory,
imitating the blue robe of Mary,
     is not too legendary

to flower both as symbol and as pungency.
Springing from stones beside the sea,

the height of Christ when thirty-three—
it feeds on dew and to the bee
"hath a dumb language"; is in reality
                a kind of Christmas-Tree.

MARIANNE MOORE

FROM THE POEM "CREATION STORY"

Vanilla
is the Emily Dickinson of orchids:
plain white flowers, yet its lush vine
can trail ten stories carried by the trees.
Green pods are cured dark walnut brown.
Sliced open lengthwise: infinitesimal seeds,
printer's ink. Their black flecks ice cream
or a sauce for pheasants or steeps in oil
where the scent lingers, like a morning moon.
The aztecs used vanilla, brewed it salty for Columbus.
It took the English to make it sweet.
A cure for impotence, they thought,
smoking it with tobacco. . . .

NATASHA SAJE

THE ELEMENTS

In most respects, the ancient world was much simpler than the modern world. In the ancient world, people recognized only four basic elements—earth, air, fire, and water—and these elements were considered not only the building blocks of the material world but also the elements of our characters and psyches. Thus, someone known to be passionate was thought to be possessed of fire and to be subject to the laws of fire. These earthly elements also had their correspondence in the heavens, and each astrological sign was—and still is—associated with earth (Capricorn, Taurus, Virgo), air (Gemini, Aquarius, Libra), fire (Leo, Sagittarius, Scorpio), or water (Pisces, Cancer, Aries).

Even though as moderns we must acknowledge the findings of science, the existence of more than 200 chemical elements, and the lack of empirical evidence connecting the affairs of people with the affairs of the stars, the language, imagery, and sense of wonder we associate with these concepts from the ancient world—with its alchemists and wizards—still capture our imaginations.

Try revisiting this simpler world by focusing on and using the ancient elements to organize a piece of fiction, a poem, or an essay.

PANNING INSTRUCTIONS

Brainstorm a list of places where you would least expect to find each of the elements, as in the example below:

Fire

- In the refrigerator
- On the palm of my hand

- In a laundry basket
- In a piano

Make up a **list** of verbs that you would least associate with each element, as in the list below:

- The water *sneezed*

- The fire *slept*

- The wind *stood* in line

Combine the places in the first step with the verbs in the second, along with other more conventional material, and **freewrite** to see where it takes you. If you find yourself delighting in the language and rhythm and imagery of what you are writing, consider shaping your freewriting into a poem; if you find yourself inventing a plot, try writing a story; and if you find yourself exploring a personal situation in a fresh way, try beginning an essay.

EXCAVATING INSTRUCTIONS

Begin a poem, story, or essay that expresses your relationship with parents, children, friends, and others using the freewriting you produced above. Feel free to mix up the elements as they suit your intentions, as Charles Jenkins does in his poem "Housefires and Homefries" (below).

NUGGETS

HOUSEFIRES AND HOMEFRIES

My mother sets little fires in my
shoes. They smolder like samovars.
It's her way of saying
stay home and wait for the glacier,
my father, man
of men. His golf bag is full
of snow. His shirts have ice cuffs
and frozen collars. My parents stare

at each other until their eyes turn
to earth and ash and when one speaks
the other blows air into paper bags
and the bags float like syllables
spoken under water.

They have filled their waterbed
with gasoline in anticipation
of making love and the obligatory
sharing of a cigarette.

I'm their little fireman who rushes in
with a garden hose
to douse them with marigolds.

CHARLES JENKINS

 **ARTIFACTS**

THE ELEMENTS

We stay in motels named
after suspect gems,
The Topaz, The Blue Ember
because we love festive ideas
that failed or fell to ruin

and nothing is as festive or failed
as small swimming pools at night,
lit and empty.
We talk ourselves into silence
then slide into the water
and sink heavy
like unidentified corpses.

Cross-legged on the bottom,
our hair billowing up
like sea plants, we try
to say things with our hands
impossible in the air.
Our lungs ache for understanding
and the rule is
that only in understanding
may we rise.

But even here we try to speak.
The syllables leave our lips
silver and perfect and silent.
They rise, one after the other, and burst
on the mercurial sky.

Then we smile a chlorine smile
and return to our element, our room
in the Irish Diamond, The Rose
Quartz, the Sleepy Sapphire.

MICHAEL C. SMITH

THE EVOLUTION OF MINI-SKILLS

Ordinarily we think of the word "skills" as applying to fairly substantial chunks of useful behavior. Common skills include the ability to write, to type, to drive a car, to operate a computer, to speak Spanish.

However, there are other behaviors that might qualify as skills, but, because they don't seem particularly useful, we never get credit for possessing them. Notice how a child develops proficiency crawling backwards or taking a block from one bucket and putting it in another.

As adults we become expert at knowing exactly how much flour equals a cup without having to measure, at jiggling the toilet handle, just so, to keep the water from running, at carrying on a phone conversation while putting away groceries and balancing a checkbook. Though perhaps minor on some scale, these are skills, nevertheless, and we should get credit for them and celebrate our competence.

PANNING INSTRUCTIONS

1. Pay close attention to your domestic behavior and the behaviors of others you may live with, and make a note of any little thing that might qualify as an unlikely and unacknowledged skill. Make a **list** of such skills.

2. Choose one or more of these skills to examine more fully in a poem, short story, or essay. Be sure to give the development of this skill respect. You may even want to give it an "epic" flavor as Bill Watkins does in "Rolling the Clothes Dryer Lint into a Ball" (page 63).

EXCAVATING INSTRUCTIONS

For an even greater challenge, think of an emotional skill you have mastered, such as denial, looking on the bright side, and so on, and write a poem, story, or essay that explores the meaning, origin, or manifestation of this skill. For an example of this challenge, notice the way Mona Simpson's character has mastered the skill of sleeping (page 64) or how the narrator of Elizabeth Bishop's poem "One Art" has conquered losing (page 64). In the brief excerpt from their essay "On Quitting," Shelly Ross and Evan Harris dignify what, for most of us, would be a failure (see page 65).

NUGGETS

ROLLING THE CLOTHES DRYER LINT INTO A BALL

How long I had thrown this lint away
Fabric of my care-worn days
Without stopping once to feel and shape
the remnants of this piebald waste

BILL WATKINS

VID KID

My grandson Nintendo plays
His fingers move faster than tiddly-winks
Which, by the way, he can't play
When it comes to dialing my phone
Again, he can't—it's not touch tone

LORRAINE SMITS

FROM THE ESSAY "ZIPPO"

I remember that as a young boy I could light a cigarette in the wind and the other boys in the neighborhood could not. So it followed that I would light a cigarette in the wind whenever I could.

I told my friends, "The secret lies in the magic of the Zippo."
Talented youngster that I was, I whipped out the Zippo so fast that the

centrifugal force alone flipped open the lid . . . against gale force winds my cupped hands kept the flame alive . . . this was my talent.

SEAN CARTER

ARTIFACTS

FROM THE NOVEL *THE LOST FATHER*

I slept, and could sleep, anywhere. Under a sheet, my limbs would move in the thick pleasure of being unseen. I could sleep most times, especially if I had something warm. I dressed in layers of cotton and would leave some piece, a sweatshirt or a T-shirt, on top of a radiator. Then I took the warm thing and hugged it in my arms by my face and before the heat drained out of it I was fast asleep. I did that in boys' apartments to help assuage the strangeness. I always woke up first in the morning.

MONA SIMPSON

ONE ART

The art of losing isn't hard to master;
so many things seem filled with the intent
to be lost that their loss is no disaster.

Lose something every day. Accept the fluster
of lost door keys, the hour badly spent.
The art of losing isn't hard to master.

Then practice losing farther, losing faster:
places, and names, and where it was you meant
to travel. None of these will bring disaster.

I lost my mother's watch. And look! My last, or
next-to-last, of three loved houses went.
The art of losing isn't hard to master.

I lost two cities, lovely ones. And, vaster,
some realms I owned, two rivers, a continent.
I miss them, but it wasn't a disaster.

Even losing you (the joking voice, a gesture
I love) I shan't have lied. It's evident

the art of losing's not too hard to master
though it may look like (*Write* it!) like disaster.

ELIZABETH BISHOP

FROM THE ESSAY "ON QUITTING"

First, the quitter thinks about quitting. This stage includes contemplating unhappiness, frustration, and shame, and dwelling on discomforts, injustices, and boredom. It can satisfy the quitter for months or even years. Next, the quitter fantasizes about methods of quitting. This is often the most creative part of the process, and many quitters draw it out, letting the imaginative quality that is inherent in many quitters come to the fore. Finally, the quitter quits.

SHELLY ROSS AND EVAN HARRIS

THE NOTE READ, "THERE ARE MORE WHERE THESE CAME FROM"

n many homes, roommates, spouses, children, and parents prepare to head out the door in several different directions at once in the morning, quickly filling each other in on the day's upcoming events while buttering their toast. Some days we may catch up by phone; other days we may find ourselves scribbling brief notes to remind a son to start dinner, a wife that we have a seven o'clock meeting, a roommate that it's her turn to take the recyclable bottles out to the curb. If we live alone, we may write notes to ourselves to help us remember deadlines, appointments, and phone calls we need to return.

While these short notes usually succeed at communicating their points when they are written, even just days later their content can seem cryptic, obscure, and baffling. The abbreviated language can also serve as creative inspiration as in the following exercise.

PANNING INSTRUCTIONS

1. Write several different short notes that you might actually leave for a person you live with or for yourself if you live alone The notes should fit into the following categories:

- **Informational** ("I'll be home late tonight"; "Help!—We're out of milk"; "I'm taping so don't turn off the VCR"; "Remember to call Jack.")

- **Emotional** ("I'm sorry I yelled this morning"; "I love you anyway"; "Let's celebrate later.")

- **Absurd** ("The cat ate the gerbil"; "I invented Pig Latin"; "You'll never win at Scrabble"; "I saw a unicorn on the Beltway this morning.")

2. Using one of these notes as a starting point, begin a poem, story, or essay that challenges our initial expectations. What does your note tell us about you? About the person you wrote it to? About the life you are living? Notice how the evocative poem "This Is Just to Say" by William Carlos Williams is an elaboration of an informational note (see page 68). Or write a piece in which you combine several of the notes in an imaginative way, as Alex McNeal does in his poem "Notes" (below).

EXCAVATING INSTRUCTIONS

Use the short note form to tell someone you live with something honest and surprising about him or yourself—for example, "I have always hated the way you make eggs"; "I love your phony English accent"; "I'm tired of washing your dirty socks"; "You look handsome when you forget to shave"; "I want a pet monkey"; "I don't want to live with you anymore." If you live alone, astonish yourself with your revelation.

Try writing a poem in note form that explores this confession. Or work on a story or essay in which this note serves as a catalyst for further insights.

NUGGETS

NOTES

Went to movies. Be back
11ish. Pick up some Lysol. Bathroom. Ugh!!!
Saw your old girl friend. Ugh!!!
We're out of beer man. How come?
Every lightbulb in this house
is out. Cool, uh?
Saw your ex again. Mind
if I call her. (Kidding.)
Why six jars of sauerkraut? Were they on sale
or have you gone funny?
I aced the psych test but I'm still
depressed.
Saw your ex again. She asked about you. Can you believe she's a Road
    Test Dummies freak?
Your mom called. No message. Sounded happy, as usual.
Your mom called again. Guess you didn't get back.

Something about your dad. Better call.
Saw Kim again. She got a tattoo on her inner thigh. How come I know
   that?
One lightbulb?? Eight rooms? Cool.

ALEX McNEAL

ARTIFACTS

THIS IS JUST TO SAY

I have eaten
the plums
that were in
the icebox

and which
you were probably saving
for breakfast

Forgive me
they were delicious
so sweet
so cold

WILLIAM CARLOS WILLIAMS

FROM THE SHORT STORY "NOTHING TO DO WITH LOVE"

I would call this all a dream, but the note she left perched for me on the
nightstand beside my bed was real. I gave it to the officer at the Bureau
of Missing Persons. He took it in his hand and acknowledged its
substance.

Mom,

   I don't expect you to understand. This has nothing to do with
love, but I'm leaving. I just had to get out of this house. Sometime
soon I'll get in touch.

   Robin

She is right: I do not understand. But she is wrong: this has
everything to do with love.

JOYCE REISER KORNBLATT

QUILTING

Even those of us who claim not to be materialistic can't help but form attachments to certain clothes. Like fragments from old songs, clothes can evoke both cherished and painful memories. A worn-thin, gauzy dress may hang in the back of a closet even though it hasn't been worn in years because the faint scent of pine that lingers on it is all that remains of someone's sixteenth summer. An impractical white muff might be pulled out of a donation bag at the last minute because of the promise of elegance it once held for its owner. And a ripped T-shirt might be rescued from the dust rag bin long after the name of the band once emblazoned across it has faded into oblivion.

Clothes document personal history for writers the same way that fossils chart time for archaeologists. In these exercises, you'll dig through your closets and drawers to explore the creative possibilities for writing that clothing can uncover.

PANNING INSTRUCTIONS

1. Root through your closet and drawers and locate clothing that was significant to you during different times in your life. (Even those who are "good" about getting rid of old clothes should find enough recent memories to complete this exercise.)

Create a **list** of the clothes that have special meaning for you.

2. Label the event(s) that each item on your list of clothing causes you to recall, as well as the feelings it evoked, as in the list below:

Clothing	Event	Feeling
Angora sweater	ice-skating party	lonely, Brian didn't show up
White bathrobe	quiet nights in my first apartment	peaceful, independent
Blue suit	job interviews	nervous, young overprepared

3. Begin a poem, story, or essay based on one or more of these items of clothing. To discover the connections that exist between the items, try dedicating a stanza or paragraph to each item and letting the relationships between the pieces unfold naturally.

If you decide to work on a poem, try creating your own quilt pattern by using the same number of lines in each stanza and beginning each stanza with the same words or structures, as in the student poem "Don't Ask Me" (see below).

EXCAVATING INSTRUCTIONS

Add to your quilt by including scraps of clothing that belong to someone who is close to you or who was *once* close to you. If their clothing actually exists in closets and drawers that are accessible, you may want to begin by selecting several pieces and labeling them as you did above. It's more likely, however, that this clothing has been stored exclusively in your mind's eye. If that's the case, sort through your memory and see what important fragments remain. Notice the power a blue jacket takes on in the poem "How It Is" by Maxine Kumin (see page 72).

NUGGETS

DON'T ASK ME

Don't ask me about the red.
The hem of the bright red orlon sweater
given me one Christmas
became hopelessly caught in a carnivorous
zipper and appalled my lovely third grade teacher.

Don't ask me about the white.
The collar of my best white shirt
should have had lipstick on it

but remained as virginal as a priest
who was really a saint.

ROBERT METTLER

WORLD QUILT

beige corduroy square of Somalia
cloth dry as the trees stripped
of leaves, stripped of bark boiled
into thin stringy soup, where hope
is diarrhea eating away the flesh
of children. O, rumpled land

worn down to the nap . . .

LORRAINE SMITS

FROM *AN IDEA SO FOREIGN,* A NOVEL IN PROGRESS

Sometimes Elaine tried on clothes late at night while the radio voices
prattled away. She had gone back to work when Terry was sixteen
months old, and over the years had amassed a substantial wardrobe.
Expert at buying expensive clothes at discount prices—she could
recognize a name brand even with three-fourths of a label cut out—
Elaine had accumulated an impressive collection of linen suits, A-line
skirts, wool slacks and silk blouses. While the cuts and fabrics of her
clothes were conservative, she favored bright, even dramatic, colors that
had made her pale skin gleam when she was younger. But the lemon
yellows, lime greens and sugar-plum pinks that had once made her feel
brisk and efficient as she clicked in her two-inch heels down the
hallway of the office where she worked, now made her skin appear
sallow and seemed to deepen the pockets under her eyes and darken
the splotches that stained her hands and forearms.

SUZANNE GREENBERG

ARTIFACTS

FROM THE POEM "ODE TO MY SOCKS"

Maru Mori brought me
a pair
of socks

which she knitted herself
with her sheep-herder's hands,
two socks as soft
as rabbits.
I slipped my feet
into them as though into
two
cases knitted
with threads of
twilight . . .

PABLO NERUDA

FROM THE POEM "HOW IT IS"

Shall I say how it is in your clothes?
A month after your death I wear your blue jacket.
The dog at the center of my life recognizes
you've come to visit, he's ecstatic.
In the left pocket, a hole.
In the right, a parking ticket
delivered up last August on Bay State Road.
In my heart, a scatter like milkweed,
a flinging from the pods of my soul.
My skin presses your old outline.
It is hot and dry inside . . .

MAXINE KUMIN

THE FAMILY NORMAL

To hear their stories, you would think that all families have black sheep, those maligned souls who fell short of or deviated from a family's cherished values or aims: the daughter who preferred tending bar to tending children, the son who broke the long line of lawyers and decided to join the Peace Corps, the nephew who loves working at the 7-Eleven, despite his Ph.D.

Often, though, the supposed rebel is in fact taking her cues from the family's unspoken values. For example, the daughter who has been shunned by her family after being fired for suspected embezzlement learned how to defraud by watching her father do his taxes. And the student who drops out of college to take care of his sick grandmother after his parents worked long hours at jobs they didn't like so he could have an education is only exemplifying what they have shown him they value: sacrifice.

In the following exercises you'll examine your family's not-so-obvious values and explore the creative potential of hidden traditions.

PANNING INSTRUCTIONS

1. For this assignment, try to discover your family's values by filling in the blanks after the following prompts:

- The event/relative my family never talks about is _____
_____ .

- The only thing my parents ever lied about was _____
_____ .

- If families could create holidays, ours would be to celebrate the day that
_____ .

- In my family, the worst thing that could happen to you is _____
_____ .

- If my family had its own coat of arms, the colors would be _____,
_____, _____, and the animal would be a
_____ .

2. Look over your responses and **freewrite** or **free associate** on some of
the values—patriotism, thrift, honesty, education—your family held (either the
family you belonged to growing up or the family you have since created on
your own). Be sure to focus not only on the values they *claim* as values, but
also those implied by gestures and behaviors. For example, several people in
a family may have filed bankruptcy. Though no one specifically advocated this
measure, filing bankruptcy became an expectation for you as an adult.

Focus on a questionable expectation or value and begin a poem, story, or
essay showing how it created conflict for an individual who "fell short." See
the excerpt from the memoir *Riding in Cars with Boys* for an example of how
an unspoken expectation—getting pregnant before marriage—can get passed
down to the next generation (see page 76).

EXCAVATING INSTRUCTIONS

Start a poem, story, or essay that spotlights one specific occasion when one of
your family's values was taken to a ludicrous or extreme level. For example,
maybe your family cherishes getting a "good deal" so much that your mother
and you spent months searching for your prom dress at yard sales before
breaking down and going to a department store. Or maybe your family values
competition so much that your children spent an entire week at the beach
indoors staging a Monopoly tournament. If you're working on a poem or
story, feel free to exaggerate the facts for effect.

In your writing, consider some of the reasons for the value being taken to
this extreme as well as the toll it might be taking on various members of the
family. For instance, perhaps children who are playing Monopoly all week at
the beach feel safer competing among each other than they do interacting with
strangers they might meet. Ultimately, isolation and loneliness might be some
of the effects of this value being taken so far. In the excerpt from "Beauty Shop,"
notice the way Joanne Bogazzi begins to examine how worrying over their
hair hides other problems that her mother and she might be sharing (see page
75).

 **NUGGETS**

FROM "BEAUTY SHOP," AN ESSAY IN PROGRESS

This was the fourth beauty shop we had visited this month, and the smell of hairspray, cigarette smoke and well-thumbed through magazines almost seemed like home to me. I saw my mother every Saturday afternoon when I picked her up from the nursing home for our weekly visit. It didn't matter that each time I came with a different plan for the afternoon—from visiting a museum to seeing a matinee to just plain going somewhere to talk—we always ended up doing the same thing, trying to find the one beautician in all of Atlanta who could meet my mother's exacting qualifications.

Hair was an obsession with her, and try as I might not to, I had inherited this unfortunate family fixation. Not that you could tell to look at me. Much to my mother's horror, I wore my own hair short and straight as a little boy's, but secretly I was as obsessed as she was with the perfect hairstyle. I was just more savvy about hiding my fixation.

I wondered lately if our obsession with the perfect hair style hid a deeper obsession, a panic that I had, and perhaps she shared, about the rest of our clearly unfocused, unexacting lives, her short, failed marriages, my sense of seemingly permanent dislocation. Even as we paid fastidious attention to the exact proportions of her haircuts, of the relationship between bangs and forehead, highlights and layers, the rest of both of our lives seemed to be drifting past us. I wanted to talk to my mother about what was inside of her; instead we focused on the outside, on the frazzled, split, overprocessed strands of her remaining hair.

JOANNE BOGAZZI

THE FAMILY NORMAL

We had snakes in our garden
because we were *that* kind of family:
cousins would change gender, aunts
would disappear on singles' cruises
through the Bermuda Triangle.

My paternal grandfather pole-vaulted
for a hobby until he was seventy,
and his wife gleefully set fires
in other people's bathrooms.

Is it any wonder I'm without wife
and credit? Yes, a wonder
because my father
before going off to a monastery
in the shadow of the French Pyrenees
said I was to be "the family normal."
Watching me protect my friends
from my relatives, he knew
I held the one chromosome
untouched by the moon. And I knew,
the morning my mother walked naked
into the A&P, I'd keep this thing to myself.

But then, they were only garter snakes,
good long sad fellows.

MICHAEL JENKINS

ARTIFACTS

FROM *RIDING IN CARS WITH BOYS: CONFESSIONS OF A BAD GIRL WHO MAKES GOOD*, A MEMOIR

My nine-year-old sister stood at the bottom of the stairs and looked up at me. "Bev?" she whispered.

I was embarrassed to meet her eyes. She looked like she might start bawling. What was I doing, banished to the stairs like a scarlet woman? What kind of an example was I setting for my sisters? You'd think I'd murdered somebody the way my parents were acting, when all I did was have sexual intercourse—and not even that often. . . .

"Your father and I have discussed this. If you want, we'll adopt it. You're too young to get married. You'll regret it for the rest of your life."

"Adopt it?" I stood up shouting. "You just want to steal my baby. I'm keeping it. I'm getting married. It's *my* baby."

"All right. All right." My father wasn't crying anymore. "You just calm down. You're underage, smart ass. You need our permission."

"I'll elope."

"You think it's fun? You think it's easy? You think that boyfriend of yours will be a good provider? You think he can keep a job and support a baby?"

"Mom was pregnant when you got married." This was my ace in the hole. I'd figured it out by subtraction, years ago. This was the first time I'd mentioned it.

"That was different," my mother said. "We were older. We knew what we were doing."

"Daddy was unemployed. You didn't have any money. You told me yourself. You lived in a shack."

"That's enough." My father stood up.

BEVERLY DONOFRIO

PHOTO ALBUM

Most of us have good intentions when it comes to organizing photographs. We purchase thick albums and plan to begin sorting through that messy drawer or box as soon as we get a little free time. Meanwhile, last year's Christmas pictures are mingling with photographs from the year before, and it's virtually impossible to tell which Thanksgiving turkey Uncle Robert is proudly basting. Photographs of new babies all begin to resemble each other, and soon we may find ourselves arguing with another family member over whether that woman wearing the striking boa is a distant relative who showed up at Grandma and Grandpa's golden wedding anniversary or a costumed attorney who danced by herself all night at a Mardi Gras party a few years back.

This exercise will be of no help to you if your goal is simply to organize your photographs. Instead, the exercise is designed to help you disorganize them even more in the hopes of making surprising new connections.

PANNING INSTRUCTIONS

1. Choose two photographs of people you know but who have never met each other. They may be the same age but on two different sides of your family; they may both be ex-boyfriends or girlfriends; or they may exist in different times entirely (for example, your deceased great grandmother and your two-year-old nephew). Beginning with their first names, **free associate** on each of the photos for five minutes. Don't be hemmed in by what you know about the people whose photos you have chosen. Instead, as with all free associations, allow the words you come up with to lead you to new discoveries.

2. Introduce these people to each other by clearing off a space on your desk or kitchen table and placing the photographs next to each other. Study the expressions on their faces. Is your father-in-law sneering at your childhood best friend, who smiles back at him oblivious? Why is your second cousin twice removed batting her eyes at your next-door neighbor, who seems to be demonstrating how to bite off a hang nail? **Freewrite** on this new relationship for ten minutes.

3. Begin a poem or story in which these two characters meet. Use what you know about their personalities as you describe the encounter, as Selma Jackson does in "I Have Married My Father's Eyes" (below). Or, if you prefer, make up character traits to enhance your poem or story.

If you'd rather work on a piece of creative nonfiction, explain why these two people should know each other, what they could add to each other's lives. You might try beginning with the line "It's too bad that _____ and _____ never met."

EXCAVATING INSTRUCTIONS

Insert yourself in your story, poem, or essay by exploring the reasons why you are bringing these two people together. What are your associations with each of them? Do they know different parts of you? Why would your life be better, more complete if they knew each other?

NUGGETS

FROM THE SHORT STORY "I HAVE MARRIED MY FATHER'S EYES"

It's something I do every five or six years: go through and try to organize photographs into their chronological sequence. The problem is that lately I don't have a ghost of an idea as to when what happened, so the challenge is to approximate our personal history as best I can. Did Frank and I go to the Grand Canyon before or after my sister Mildred graduated from college? Were we descending the canyon walls on burros before Eddie took this picture of his daughter playing the role of Martha in *Who's Afraid of Virginia Woolf?* Had we already gazed upon the surreal oddness of the London Bridge in Lake Havasu City, Arizona, by the time that picture of Frank in his new snorkeling goggles was taken? Beats me. And here, what's this picture of my father doing right next to Frank's picture? Now there would be a meeting! If my father had been alive when I met and started going out with Frank, all hell would have been paid. And yet in some ways—in ways they would never acknowledge—they are alike. Dad rarely said anything twice; ditto for Frank. Hell, Frank rarely says anything once.

Selma Jackson

 **ARTIFACTS**

Brothers & Sisters

1

Even among your family you stand off to one side,
your big, dead face at last benign. The picture's
not dated, but everybody's poormouthed, pale, sun-
in-the-eye, the background data circa nineteen
sixty-nine. The photography functional. Your sisters look like part of the
    class, your
brothers part of the company. With some formality
each of you holds your own other hand. You're
practically the parent here, though it's Paul
who's about to complain to the camera: the angle's wrong,
too much sun. Everybody's blue or brown suit is shining.

2

We're out of the movies. The pictures don't lie,
Vivien Leigh is snow white Blanche DuBois. She has
a sister, the one everybody says you look like.
It is nineteen fifty-one, summer, and out on the sidewalk
the mere sun is blinding, tag-end. This is the matinee.

I saw you naked once, the lady at her bath. It's true,

you looked like somebody else. I had never seen so much
flesh. I ran the movie over and over. Pictures don't lie.
In the fifties photograph you still look like somebody's
brilliant sister, the girl in time, all face, too beautiful
but good, who's doting too completely on the boy.

3

In school we were told to draw our parents. Everybody
made moons—great pumpkin smiling moons, vegetable moons,
elliptical moons, moons like sad maps, eyes, ears, nose,

and chinless moons. We even cut black paper for cameos.
All of the faces floated in the dead air of pictures.

For years now their faces have run together. My father's
lives in my mother's as if by blood. Brother and sister.
She looks down at me from the dream as through a mirror.
She has the face of a child, somebody small, lunar.
Somebody's always standing by the bed. Sleep is the story

in which the child falls to the dead, rises, and is loved.

Stanley Plumly

PRODUCT WARNINGS

To look at the warnings printed on virtually every product we buy, it would be fair to say that we consume at our own risk. While the many warning labels on a ladder, for example, are undoubtedly the fruit of liability suits, it is nevertheless unsettling to see them all there in yellow and red telling us not to "use on ice" or "lean against a power line."

Product warnings have their own clipped style. For example, a can of shaving cream shouts CONTENTS UNDER PRESSURE, rather than "The contents of this can are under pressure." When looked at with a writer's perspective, the gravity and drama of some of these warnings can be suggestive of other forms of creative writing. The following exercises ask you to play with these product warnings and to see what might come from them.

PANNING INSTRUCTIONS

Look at several product containers and instructions and make a **list** of warnings you find. Try mixing and matching some of the warnings in bizarre and humorous ways. See if you can write several sentences composed only of warnings, and be alert to possibilities for further development as poems, stories, or essays.

EXCAVATING INSTRUCTIONS

Take this exercise a step further by exploring what happens when warnings are not heeded, as George Irving does in "Federal Offenses" (page 84). Consider also writing a love poem using only warnings, as in the poem "She Should Have Come with Warnings" (page 83).

 **NUGGETS**

Shawn Hall's poem "She Should Have Come with Warnings" (see below) developed out of the following list:

WARNING/CAUTION	PRODUCT
Use gentle strokes with a sharp razor. Contents under pressure. Do not puncture or incinerate. Do not heat for warm lather or any other purpose.	**Barbasol**
If rash or irritation develops, discontinue use. Do not apply to broken or irritated skin.	**Shower To Shower** (deodorant body powder)
Avoid spraying in eyes. Keep out of reach of children. Intentional misuse by deliberately concentrating and inhaling the contents can be harmful or fatal.	**Aqua Net** (hair spray)
Keep Away From Water Do not use while bathing. Always "Unplug It" after use	**Vidal Sassoon Cold Shot 1500 Hair Dryer**
May explode or leak, and cause burn injury, if recharged, disposed in a fire, mixed with different battery type, inserted backwards or disassembled.	**Duracell Batteries**
Burned out bulbs should be replaced quickly. Several burned out bulbs left in this set may cause the other bulbs to heat up and burn out.	**Good Tidings Xmas Tree Lights**

■

SHE SHOULD HAVE COME WITH WARNINGS

Her eyes were as green
as the modern world
and just as toxic

when she cried. She should have come
with warnings.
When the rash
developed, I tried to discontinue
use, but by then
several bulbs had burned out
and I could not replace them.
The contents of her thoughts seemed always
under pressure. I thought they might
explode or leak
and cause burn injuries. Do not
puncture or incinerate, I thought.
Do not apply to broken skin.

Once she called me at work
in the middle of the day
to say only that she had drawn
a picture of my right hand
from a memory. Which one, I said,
but she hung up. Always unplug
after use. Use gentle strokes
with a sharp razor. Misuse may result
in sickness or death. She should have come
with warnings.

Shawn Hall

ARTIFACTS

From the short story "Federal Offenses"

Already I was an hour late for work. Taft would assume I had one of those epic *Lost Weekends* and was writhing under the spell of toxic DTs.

I lay there hugging my pillow, annoyed at myself for oversleeping and annoyed at the stiff tag protruding from under the pillowcase and scratching my cheek. **Under Penalty of Law This Tag Is Not To Be Removed,** it read. The tag tried to assure me that all new material consisted of polyester fiber. And then in very fine print, it listed statute codes and stamps from six different states, including the District of Columbia.

I tried to rip the tag off, but it was double stitched into the seam. I gave it another tug, and it came off, along with batting from the pillow and foam pellets. "Great. I killed the pillow," I said aloud, and strangely I felt that something of that order had happened, especially as the foam pellets continued to seep out. All the sleep that had taken place on those pellets, all the dreams they had absorbed. . . .

GEORGE IRVING

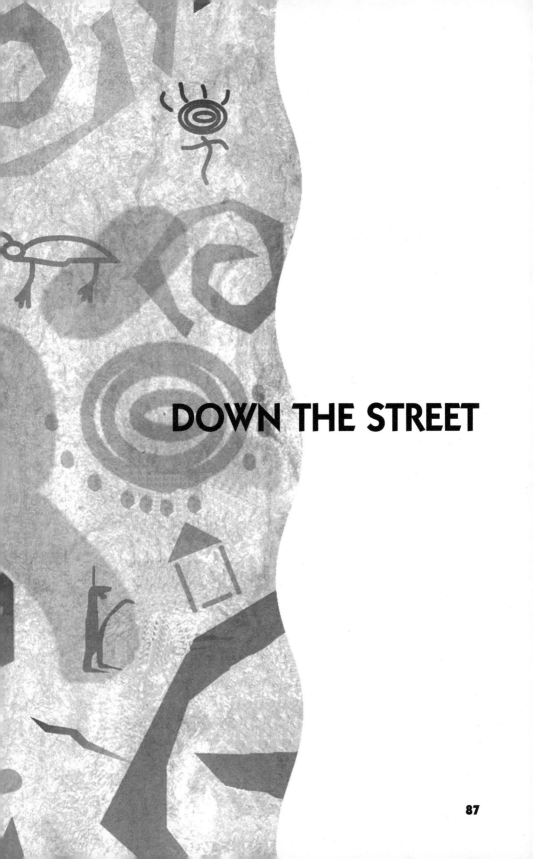

DOWN THE STREET

GETTING LOST, FINDING THE WAY

Most of us have gotten lost on our way somewhere, whether to a place local or distant. Maybe you got lost one day taking a shortcut through your own familiar neighborhood or, more typically, found yourself wandering in circles through a strange and distant city. The experience of getting lost is inherently dramatic, regardless of how long it takes to find the way. Indeed, getting lost and finding the way is one of life's basic dramas.

PANNING INSTRUCTIONS

Begin a poem, story, or piece of creative nonfiction about a time you got lost. Consider the whole experience: the point at which you realized you were lost (even before that: were there signs or forebodings that you might get lost?) and what you saw and experienced while you were lost and when you eventually found your way. To help you generate material, complete or develop with details the following statements:

1. Things weren't right even before I left (describe the "things").

2. I knew I was lost when . . .

3. I was lost, and to make matters worse . . .

4. If I hadn't gotten lost, I would (not) have . . .

5. While I was trying to find the way, I kept thinking . . .

Combine your responses, as Lorraine Smits did in "No Time" (page 89), and consider possible meanings of why you got lost. Maybe some part of you knew exactly what you were doing. Perhaps you weren't lost at all.

EXCAVATING INSTRUCTIONS

Try doing the same exercise metaphorically. Instead of being lost with respect to an actual place, consider experiences where you were intellectually lost or emotionally lost or spiritually lost. In the poem "This Is the Way" (on page 91), the last stanza suggests that the "founding fathers" were morally lost as well as geographically lost. Try using some of the same details and expressions from the first exercise.

NUGGETS

FROM THE SHORT STORY "NO TIME"

Fog swirled around. So thick at times even the white line on the road disappeared. You'll see signs, the man at the gas station had said. I had used up an eighth of a tank of gas and seen no sign. Wait! The fog wasn't quite so dense. Something was forming up ahead. A road sign. It looked so strange, though. A pale purple, almost pink. Points all around the edges like a misshapen star. The words were black and seemed to leap out—*You Are Here*. Here? Where is *Here?* I felt confused, the way I did last week in the Metro Station. I had stood in front of the map board trying to figure out which exit I wanted. The bright red star saying *You Are Here* hadn't helped at all. I still took the wrong escalator and walked blocks out of my way.

This road was so dark. When the fog was patchy, I saw trees crowding the sides, thick and woodsy. At times bare branches seemed to reach out and gather in the fog. It's a shortcut, the man had said. But the gas gauge had dropped below the halfway mark. Why does the unfamiliar seem so much longer and darker? My radio had shorted out on the way to the party. Took the clock with it. No friendly green eye to keep me company. No soothing voice to calm my uneasiness.

LORRAINE SMITS

ARTIFACTS

FROM THE SHORT STORY "A GOOD MAN IS HARD TO FIND"

They turned onto the dirt road and the car raced roughly along in a swirl of pink dust. The grandmother recalled the times when there were no paved roads and thirty miles was a day's journey. The dirt road was hilly and there were sudden curves on dangerous embankments. All at once they would be on a hill, looking down over the blue tops of trees for miles around, then the next minute, they would be in a red depression with the dust-coated trees looking down on them.

"This place had better turn up in a minute," Bailey said, "or I'm going to turn around."

FLANNERY O'CONNOR

FROM THE MEMOIR *REMEMBERING THE BONE HOUSE*

Another day, Sally and I get lost in earnest. We've been mistreated by one or more of the women in that high white house, each of whom confers power on the others, and for once we're making good on our threat to run away. We stomp right off Lindall Hill and into town. This would have been the familiar territory of Mother's adolescence, which I will read about in a few years, during my own adolescence, in a diary she lets me see. She walked to high school through these streets, and wandered through them after school with her friends, especially her boyfriend Darren, whom she might have married, thereby eradicating me from her future and my own tenuous present. . . . Sally and I wander past streets of houses and on into the business district, clutching hands, increasingly confused and nervous. Being together protects us from panic, however, as though we can never go really, truly irrevocably astray in the world unless we lose each other. We're even a little titillated to be having the experience we've so often been warned against: Getting Lost.

NANCY MAIRS

THIS IS THE WAY

We are only a little
lost. Any minute
our destination will appear
around the next hill, past one more
light. Let's just see. Sure

we could clear this up
at the Texaco station on the corner
but doing so lacks gusto and style.
If we have to ask others in times
like this, where are we? More lost
than we are now, I say, even though we're

hours late and haven't seen asphalt in miles,
even though we're running out of gas
and the passengers are skeletons
who died of uremic poisoning
when their bladders burst. Still

this is the best method. This
is the way our fathers
and forefathers, lost for months
crazed with their own conversations
drinking salt water and eating
their slaves, found America.

MICHAEL C. SMITH

EFFECTS AND SIDE EFFECTS

odern science has blessed us with drugs to cure and combat hundreds of diseases and conditions, and every day yet another "miracle" drug is announced. The downside of many of the medications prescribed for us is that they often have side effects nearly as uncomfortable as the condition from which we seek relief. And sometimes the treatments of the side effects lead to a chain reaction that makes us ask whether the problem is as bad as the cure. For example, a medication for high blood pressure produces an upset stomach. So the doctor prescribes another medication for the upset stomach, which produces headaches and sleeplessness. Yes, the blood pressure has been treated, but . . .

PANNING INSTRUCTIONS

Try your hand at inventing a chain reaction of side effects. Or choose to use actual warnings you may have been given by a doctor or pharmacist. Begin with completing the following warning: "This drug will certainly take care of the __(problem)__; however, it has a couple of unfortunate side effects:

Try filling in the following blanks with expected and unexpected details—for example, "You may feel a burning sensation in your checking account."

1. You may feel a _____ in your _____.

2. Your _____ will probably hurt.

3. In the morning, you may experience _____ or _____.

4. Don't be surprised if your _____ begins to _____.

5. If your _____ throbs, take a teaspoon of _____, though this may _____ until _____.

Use the material you generate here to help you begin a poem, story, or essay in which the medical side effects cause significant problems. In the prose poem by James Tate, "Distance from Loved Ones" (page 94), a woman pays for cosmetic surgery with a "sad" sequence of side effects.

EXCAVATING INSTRUCTIONS

Prescription drugs are not the only remedies that have side effects. Anytime we attempt to solve a problem, there is the possibility that the solution may create more—and perhaps worse—problems than the original: we attempt to fix the toilet and convert a small leak into a torrent; a friend takes our advice about how to end a relationship, and we are suddenly thrust in the middle of it, making everything worse.

Work on a poem, narrative, or essay in which the attempts to solve a problem actually create more problems. Use the following prompts to get you started:

1. As though _____ weren't already bad enough, I had to make things worse by _____.

2. I managed to fix the _____, but in the process I _____.

3. Sure, I had a brand new _____, but I also had the worst case of _____ you've ever seen.

 **NUGGETS**

FROM A SHORT STORY IN PROGRESS

As though having to flee to Mexico weren't bad enough, I had to make things worse by mouthing off to the customs agent. When he asked if we had anything to declare, I blurted, "I declare my love for freedom and independence. Viva Las Vegas!"

And that customs agent would have none of that. He whipped open the car door, grabbed me by the ear, led my body from the car and cursed at me, his spit jettisoning like small comets into my eyes. In short, he detained me.

SEAN CARTER

ARTIFACTS

FROM THE POEM "DISTANCE FROM LOVED ONES"

After her husband died, Zita decided to get the face-lift she had always wanted. Halfway through the operation, her blood pressure started to drop, and they had to stop. When Zita tried to fasten her seat-belt for the sad ride home, she threw out her shoulder. . . .

JAMES TATE

CAUGHT UP IN THE NEWS

Daily we are bombarded by news from myriad sources—newspapers, magazines, TV, radio, Internet. We absorb much more information than we can possibly use, and all the irrelevant information gets mixed up with the relevant. Why do we need to know about another car accident, murder, wonderful accomplishment by a celebrity athlete, or the passage of a bill that affects six people in Alaska?

The following exercises encourage you to make creative use of all this news by incorporating it in your own writing—to indeed look for more news and use it in creative ways.

PANNING INSTRUCTIONS

Look through several issues of newspapers and magazines and copy down leads and headlines that strike you as provocative, amusing, or absurd. Link the leads together in semi-logical ways. For example, Anita Perez took the following leads from the July 6, 1994, edition of *The Washington Post* and produced the plausible sentences below to begin a story:

The all talk, no help labels on bottles
U.S. to bar Haitians picked up at sea
Labrador lovers unleash their anger
Battered woman's cry relayed up from grass roots
Bus repair pact scrapped
Boy devours books
What Popeye didn't know
Name two sports with no clear goals

> *The women unleashed their anger because the United States barred the all talk, no help labels on Haitians.*

Popeye didn't know that devouring books is better than devouring grass roots and spinach.

The bus of battered labradors was scrapped because it had no clear goals.

She chose the first sentence to help her begin her story about two women who meet while waiting to see their senators (see below).

EXCAVATING INSTRUCTIONS

Combine excerpts from several stories in different newspapers and magazines in a story, poem, or essay. Feel free to add your own connections and language. Notice how the excerpt from Ron Carlson's story, "Reading the Paper" (below), creates a strange effect by combining ordinary, daily details and behaviors with details drawn from the newspaper.

NUGGETS

FROM A STORY IN PROGRESS

Two women, who did not know each other, met outside of Senator Bradley's office to unleash their anger about the administration's policy toward Haitians. They were particularly upset about all the talk and the lack of aid. The women didn't know that the senator was in Colorado. In the course of the five hours they waited, they got to know each other quite well. . . .

ANITA PEREZ

ARTIFACTS

FROM THE STORY "READING THE PAPER"

All I want to do is read the paper, but I've got to do the wash first. There's blood all over everything. Duke and the rest of the family except me were killed last night by a drunk driver, run over in a movie line, and this blood is not easy to get out. Most of the fabrics are easy to clean, however, so I don't even bother reading the fine print on the Cheer box. They make this soap to work in all conditions anymore.

Then I get Timmy up and ready for school. He eats two Hostess doughnuts and before he's even down the street and I've picked up the paper, I can hear him screaming down there. Somebody's dragging him into a late model Datsun, light brown, the kind of truck Duke, bless his soul, always thought was silly. So, I've got the paper in my hands and there's someone at the door. So few people come to the back door that I know it's going to be something odd, and I'm right. It's that guy in the paper who escaped from prison yesterday. He wants to know if he can come in and rape me and cut me up a little bit. Well, after he does that, my coffee's cold, so I pour a new cup. . . .

RON CARLSON

NEIGHBORLY AND UNNEIGHBORLY NEIGHBORS

With the fragmentation of our culture and its inherent value of individualism and privacy, the status and role of our neighbors are by no means assured. For all those who like and trust their neighbors and consider them beloved relatives, there are just as many who keep a safe and frosty distance from them, fearing that they will borrow and break the lawn mower or want to know more about our lives than they have a right to.

Regardless of where we fall on this issue, there are things each of us would do with our neighbors and things each of us most emphatically would not do, all for reasons as personal as they are logical. "Good fences make good neighbors," said Robert Frost, and when those fences, both physical and psychological, are violated, conflicts arise.

In this next exercise, you're asked to examine those fences and explore the feelings associated with them and with the fact that we all live next to someone, whether that person is in the next apartment or next farm over from us.

PANNING INSTRUCTIONS

1. Make a **list** of items you would never lend to a neighbor, mixing the typical with the bizarre—for example, my razor, my car, my shoes, my underwear, my husband.

2. Write a piece in which you are asked and actually lend one of the bizarre items to the neighbor. Discuss the shape this item was in before you lent it and the shape it was in when it was returned. For an essay approach to this exercise, recall a time a neighbor actually asked to borrow something you weren't completely comfortable lending.

EXCAVATING INSTRUCTIONS

1. Sometimes our neighbors create other kinds of conflicts for us. They park a new BMW in their driveway and suddenly our Subaru looks old and ragged. Our carefully transplanted azaleas all die while their rhododendrons cause people to slow down and gawk. Write a piece that takes off on the theme of "Keeping Up with the Joneses" the way that Raymond Carver does in the first paragraph of his short story "Neighbors" (see page 101). Explore the tension that arises from falling behind the Joneses in some area, perhaps in an absurd way. ("We didn't even own an artist, much less a celebrity, so when the Wilsons bought Madonna and brought her home, we hid our faces and vowed to catch up.")

2. Write a piece written from the point of view of a neighbor and explore some of the conclusions the neighbor might make about you and your family.

3. Begin a poem, story, or essay about a neighbor whose actions and behavior are mysterious in some way. For example, what questions would naturally arise in the situation described in the poem "Duplex" by James Washington (page 100)?

NUGGETS

NEITHER A BORROWER NOR A LENDER BE

my neighbor says may i borrow your
guillotine this evening   i'm
having a party i need
something to amuse the guests

i have i don't mind saying
the keenest guillotine
on the block but
i'm canny   who

'll be using it i said
not
that thickneck brotherinlaw of yours
who broke my radial arm saw trimming
his leg

he never meant it
my neighbor whines   how
would he know that bone
would be so tough   and furthermore

i said i just had
that guillotine in the shop she's
not so young anymore   only
licensed operators he insists (unlike

that incident with my B-17 bomber
and his dirtbag
cousin from the eastern shore)   no
hotdogging it i exhort   we

put up the garage door
and wheel that beauty
into the midday sun   and
back tomorrow morning ten o'clock

sharp

which he does
all clean and oiled along
with brotherinlaw's soccerball
head

on my mother's
best china plate

Liz Enagonio

■

Duplex

The man next door keeps kicking
at the wall we have in common.
There is a rhythm to it, faster
than raindrops, slower
than heartbeats. At first I thought
it was a code, but the intervals
are so regular that if it is a code
he is saying the same thing over and over.
Given the conditions of this duplex, he
is probably repeating in code the name
of his god. I would complain
but the rent is low,
and anyway I've gotten caught up

in the rhythm. If my life were a scull,
the pounding on the wall would tell me
when to rest and when to row.

JAMES WASHINGTON

 **ARTIFACTS**

FROM THE SHORT STORY "NEIGHBORS"

Bill and Arlene Miller were a happy couple. But now and then they felt
they alone among their circle had been passed by somehow, leaving Bill
to attend to his bookkeeping duties and Arlene occupied with secretarial
chores. They talked about it sometimes, mostly in comparison with the
lives of their neighbors, Harriet and Jim Stone. It seemed to the Millers
that the Stones lived a fuller and brighter life. The Stones were always
going out for dinner, or entertaining at home, or traveling about the
country somewhere in connection with Jim's work.

RAYMOND CARVER

FROM THE SHORT STORY "THE NEIGHBOR"

Country people can forgive madness, but a week ago, the family's one
immediate neighbor, a dour young man in his twenties, had walked out
his back door and had seen, for the tenth time, one of their chickens
scratching in his pathway to the woodpile. He'd rushed back into the
house, and returning with an Army .45 handgun, had fired eight bullets
into the chicken, making a feathered, bloody mess.

RUSSELL BANKS

CUSTOMS AND THE CUSTOMARY

I n parts of Spain, when a person compliments someone on a possession, say a large watercolor hanging on the wall, the host/owner may offer the possession to the guest. If the guest politely declines the offer, the host may insist all the more and take it as an insult if the guest does not accept. In Japan, it is considered the height of rudeness to touch a stranger's head. In the United States, strangers will often inquire about each other's occupation as a way of breaking the ice. These are all examples of customs, habitual or ritualized behaviors practiced by discrete groups, and they may or may not have any basis in reason or rationality. And since there is no necessary connection between customs and reason, this is an area rich for creative writing possibilities.

PANNING INSTRUCTIONS

1. Select a few of the following areas and generate a **list** or try **clustering** on customs associated with each:

- Eating/Meals/Restaurants
- Public Transportation
- Weddings
- Parties
- Funerals
- Public Restrooms
- Holidays
- Greetings
- Farewells

- Sporting Events

- Dress/Fashion

- Romance

- Kissing (see the example essay on page 104)

2. Begin a poem, story, or essay that involves conflicts related to these customs, for example, the man from Albania who gets in a crowded elevator and faces rearward for twelve floors. Or consider the kind of trouble a man might get into by not observing the custom of kissing a woman's hands, a custom Michael T. Kaufman's essay challenges (page 104).

EXCAVATING INSTRUCTIONS

Try your hand at inventing your own customs for some of the areas mentioned above. Remember: these customs don't need to make any sense. Use the customs you invent in a poem, story, or essay. Notice how Dorothy Nims's poem "My House" blends and takes off on actual customs (below).

NUGGETS

MY HOUSE

In my house you must remove your shoes
and place them on your hands. Once
conversation begins, you may drop one
at a time to punctuate what
you are saying. In my house

you must try to draw a picture of me
and tell me why this is how you see me.
(All such efforts hang on the Great Wall, signed
and dated.) Here, no mention is ever made
of presidents, dead or living. You are expected
to rise when I rise, place a hand on my shoulder
and walk with me to the bathroom. In my house
the most venerable custom is the great dance
that takes places upon leaving: we embrace
as in a tango, re-trace our steps and conversations

and move out the house, where I stop
turn, and you are
gone.

DOROTHY NIMS

# ARTIFACTS

FROM THE ESSAY "KISSING CUSTOMS"

I returned not long ago from a three-year assignment in Poland, where
men kiss the hands of women as a matter of course when they meet.
When I first arrived in Warsaw, I did not think this was such a great
idea. At the time I thought of myself as a democratic kid from the streets
of New York, and the notion of bending over and brushing my lips over
the back of a woman's hand struck me as offensively feudal and
hopelessly effete. Each time some perfectly fine woman offered me the
back of her hand to kiss, I stammered my apology, saying something
like, "Gosh, no offense intended, but where I come from we don't carry
on like this, and while I respect you enormously, can't we make do with
a simple handshake?"

MICHAEL T. KAUFMAN

FIRST TIMES

The first time we do anything of significance we are usually nervous, anxious, and awkward. Whether it's our first time driving a car with a stick shift or our first date, we are like children in a sense, and we express the energy of children. We may find ourselves enthusiastic and frightened at once, headstrong and shy about whatever new adventure we have begun.

Some first times stay with us without effort on our part. We tend to remember our first loves, our first cars, and perhaps our first best friends. But other first times slip by without much fanfare; perhaps we are not even fully conscious that they are first times. Who remembers the first time she saw an R-rated movie or the first time he called an adult by her first name? In this exercise, we'll explore the way writing about first times can lend a fresh energy to your work.

OPENING INSTRUCTIONS

1. Freewrite for five minutes on four or five of the following topics that apply to your life:

- My first date

- My first airplane trip

- My first taste of Mexican food

- My first trip to the dentist

- My first prom

- My first poem

- My first love

- My first time drinking too much

- The first cake (pie, souffle) I made

- My first adult betrayal

- My first bra (suit)

- My first job interview

- My first pet

- The first lemon (kiwi, oyster) I ever tasted

- My first time living away from home

2. Spend a few minutes reading over your freewriting. Circle any words or phrases that surprise or delight you. Choose the "first time" that you most want to work on and begin a short story, poem, or essay based on this first experience.

EXCAVATING INSTRUCTIONS

1. Make your own **list** of first times. Karen Ransom, for instance, writes an essay about buying her first—and last—suit (page 107). Avoid repeating any of the items from the list in the Planning exercise. Try to include both actual events and more abstract first times as in the sample list below:

- My first real piece of jewelry (the ring Jim's mom gave me)

- The first song lyrics I memorized ("Hey Jude")

- The first time I understood what hate was (feelings for neighbor who poisoned our cat)

- My first real confrontation with an authority figure (shop teacher in eighth grade)

2. Record any memories that come to mind about each first time. Try to remember the concrete details (those involving the senses: smell, taste, touch, sight, sound) surrounding each.

Work on a story, poem, or essay in which you explore one of these experiences in more depth. Notice the way Kate Chopin's character experiences a new feeling for the first time—freedom—in the short story "The Story of an Hour" (see page 107).

NUGGETS

FROM THE ESSAY "MY FIRST SUIT"

Several months after my marriage ended, my savings account began to become so depleted, I decided to do something I had vowed I would never do: get a real job. I was twenty-nine, and I had managed to live on the kind of part-time work that didn't interfere with what I considered my "real" work, which was painting. I hadn't realized how much being married, specifically how much my husband's solid government salary, was supporting my painting until he was gone. For the moment, I needed to be self-sufficient more than I needed to be an artist, so off I went with my best friend in search of the perfect interview suit.

She led me into a shopping mall I generally studiously avoided because its artificial light and artificially made-up sales clerks depressed me and made me feel shabby. But I didn't complain. Nor did I complain or protest when she declared the third suit I tried on—a stiff blue blazer and skirt that made me feel like a flight attendant—absolutely perfect. This was my first suit, and fortunately, it turned out, my last, and it had nothing to do with me at all.

KAREN RANSOM

ARTIFACTS

FROM THE SHORT STORY "THE STORY OF AN HOUR"

There was something coming to her and she was waiting for it, fearfully. What was it? She did not know; it was too subtle and elusive to name. But she felt it, creeping out of the sky, reaching toward her through the sounds, the scents, the color that filled the air.

Now her bosom rose and fell tumultuously. She was beginning to recognize this thing that was approaching her, and she was striving to beat it back with her will—as powerless as her two white slender hands would have been.

When she abandoned herself a little whispered word escaped her slightly parted lips. She said it over and over under her breath: "free, free, free!"

KATE CHOPIN

"I WOULD HAVE BURNED MY HAIR FOR THAT WAITRESS"

Occupying a place between lovers and parents, our good friends know how to see the world the way we see it and know when that vision is distorted. It is their job to provide reality checks—to let us know, for example, that the bellbottoms don't evoke the charm of the flower age, as the salesperson led us to believe, or to dull the glitz on that no-load mutual fund we've been thinking of trading our profit sharing for.

Truly good friends hold a position of utter trust because they like us for who we are, and they don't usually have as great a stake as lovers and parents in making us feel good for the sake of feeling good or making us feel bad because whatever action we have taken or are considering taking might have a direct effect on their lives.

Trust between friends is for some nearly sacred, and when that trust is broken, when a friend tells a shared secret or offers us purposely poor advice, our feeling of betrayal does not usually fade easily. While our friends can be our greatest allies, they can also become our most difficult rivals as we test the confines of these relationships and measure our own successes and failures in relationship to theirs.

PANNING INSTRUCTIONS

1. Cluster on the words *friendship* and *trust*. Combine your "balloons" in a variety of ways in an attempt to make surprising connections.

2. Begin a story, poem, or essay involving a secret or a specific trust between two friends—you and a friend, people you know, or fictional characters. The secret should challenge the boundaries of the friendship in some way. You might explore a time that you told a confidence to a friend as a way of testing the level of this friendship, or you might write about a time that a friend became less of a friend by breaking an important trust or more of a friend by keeping a trust. Notice how a friendship is affirmed when one friend lies for another in "A Year of Living Stupidly" (see below).

EXCAVATING INSTRUCTIONS

While we usually trust our friends to be tactfully honest with us, they may not always live up to our expectations. Jealousy may cause a friend to tell you that your hair looks terrific dyed black when in fact you look like Morticia Addams on a bad day. A sense of competition may cause you to fail to remind a friend to study for an upcoming quiz.

Work on a story, essay, or poem about a time when either a friend's lack of honesty or your lack of honesty toward a friend caused a conflict in your life. The conflict may have been external (causing a fight between the two of you or others) or may have remained internal (causing you guilt or anxiety).

NUGGETS

TAKING ORDERS

I would have burned my hair
for this waitress, so full and good
were her thoughts, so tempered
her voice, and my friend knew this, so that

when I ordered the coffee
and she asked "Will there be
anything else?" my friend
answered for me so I wouldn't have
to stutter my "no thanks"
and spend all day collecting myself.

MARTIN RODRIGUEZ

■

FROM THE SHORT STORY "A YEAR OF LIVING STUPIDLY"

Those last few weeks in Viet Nam were the hardest. I totally bought into the fear that afflicted most short timers: that Charlie knew when you were shipping out and waited for your year in hell to almost end before pulling your number. So I spent a lot of time in the mortar bunker. Telford knew I was scared shitless and would take over for me on the radios when terror so seized me that I couldn't function. And when Sarge asked him where I was, he'd tell him stories—that I was in Phu Heip getting supplies or at the Korean command post dropping off bombing reports. Two days before I shipped out, the Sarge wandered into the bunker around noon, and saw me squatting there among those mildewed sandbags. He said, "You know, your friend Telford thinks you're in the village. Better tell him you're down here."

They all knew what I was going through. Everybody fell victim to superstition the last weeks. And that was okay.

MIKE BRITZ

 **ARTIFACTS**

BUDDIES

If you saw us talking in a crowded bar, knees touching,
Leaning to whisper, you'd probably think *lovers*, but no,
She likes women. She's talking along like my best buddy

With great delight, some decorum, and as the conversation
Escalates with the Scotch, I get incredibly curious,
And ask for more, to imagine one female body against another.

"The plump one," she says, "and the one with the shoe,"
And then it all goes blank. "Now tell me," she says, "it's only fair,"
And despite myself I'm confiding, whispering the good parts,

She's laughing, I'm taking in her hair, her perfume
Which doesn't end but flowers in a touching muskiness.
My whispers draw her closer. Her blouse flutters

In the bar's smoky chatter. She holds her breath
So I can see into the narrow width that represents
Our differences. She rears her head back and she roars.

STEVE ORLEN

COMMUNITY SERVICE

How many times do we hear of some famous person being sentenced to 300 hours of community service for reckless driving or 80 hours of community service for getting into a fist fight in a restaurant in front of twelve camera crews?

Some of us serve our communities out of pride and perhaps even love for our neighborhoods and neighbors. We enthusiastically run for city offices and volunteer at recreation centers and schools. Still, the majority of us find ourselves sentenced in some way to community service, if not officially by the law, then unofficially by friends and circumstances that demand our involvement.

While community involvement is certainly a good thing (it could even be argued that our neighborhoods only really exist because some citizens have it in them to start newsletters, organize block parties, and maintain neighborhood watch programs), community projects also bring out a certain zeal in some that can be overwhelming. No matter how burdened we may feel by their presence and requests for assistance, when we encounter those who possess this zeal, the interactions we have are rife with creative possibilities.

PANNING INSTRUCTIONS

1. Think back to a time when someone asked you to get involved in a neighborhood or civic cause. Perhaps a dorm-mate tried to enlist your help in setting up a building security plan or a neighbor asked you to sign a petition to get a traffic light installed. Or in the fifth grade you somehow found yourself volunteering as a crossing guard for a month. **Freewrite** about this service, generating all the details you can remember about it and the invitation to get involved. If you are now heavily involved in neighborhood causes, choose one or two that you are most active in and trace your involvement.

2. Recall the person who asked you to become involved or with whom you closely work in your community project. What physical traits (for example, tall and thin, slightly crossed eyes) and personality markers (such as eager laugh, twitchy eyebrow) does she possess? List all that you can recall.

3. Work on a story, poem, or essay that explores your encounter with community involvement. If you're working on fiction, feel free to alter and add characters. If you're working on an essay, try sorting through your motives for either getting involved or not getting involved. Mine the material for possible dramatic and comic potential, as Shirley Hickman does in her story "Neighborhood Watch" (below).

EXCAVATING INSTRUCTIONS

Just as we serve or neglect our communities, our communities can serve us or fail to serve us in crucial ways. In one neighborhood, mail may be delivered irregularly without explanation; in another, the police may seem to spend their time reading magazines at the 7-Eleven instead of patrolling the streets. While we may be annoyed at the inconveniences caused by whatever disservice we experience, irritation can be turned into creative energy.

Begin a story, poem, or essay about a time that you experienced an interruption or complication in whatever community service you had come to expect in your life—perhaps the garbage collectors went on strike or the newspaper deliverer didn't wrap your paper in plastic when it rained—or maybe several services went haywire at the same time. Whatever the incident you choose to focus on, be sure to explore any comic or other emotional potential.

NUGGETS

From the story in progress "Neighborhood Watch"

"But I don't know anything about suspicious characters," I told Irene.

She assured me I didn't need to know much and that mainly we just drove around in the wee hours in a warm jeep with a two-way radio.

"Usually," she said, "we don't see anything except maybe a family of raccoons invading a garbage can. They're very cute."

"How 'wee'?" I asked.

"Between midnight and three, and it's only once a month."

"Just to report raccoons?"

"Oh," said Irene, smiling. "Sometimes we call in husbands late in getting home."

"Is that legal?" I asked.

"I don't know," Irene confessed. "But it sure is fun."

SHIRLEY HICKMAN

POWER LINES

The year they stopped trimming back the trees
you moved away. I couldn't see you go through
the leaves but there had been rumors about it.
We all worried about power line
fires after you left. The children who played
in your deserted front yard lost kites
in the branches. When the new family moved in
none of us invited them over. I'm sorry I
didn't go to his funeral. I have a photograph
from before it happened. My kids on his lap—
the neighborhood's Grandpop. If you left a
forwarding address, I'd be happy to send it.

DELORES QUIGLEY

 **ARTIFACTS**

FROM THE SHORT STORY "THE LONGEST DAY OF THE YEAR"

Toward the end of my third marriage, when my husband and I had enough problems on our hands, the Welcome Wagon lady began to call on us. It was just a rented house—more than we could afford, too, so we were going to have to give it up before summer was over. The first time she came I told her it was an inconvenient time to talk, and that we were going to be moving, anyway. Still, she came back the next day, saying that she hoped I had a minute. That day had been hell. . . . I had to tell her that it wasn't a good time. Not to be put off, she asked when it would be. . . .

The next week she came back. She was a tall woman, quite heavy, wearing a white poncho with black stars woven into the wool and ratty-looking fur tails. She had on a black skirt that I knew the dog would get hairs all over, and a ring on her wedding finger that looked like something Richard Burton would have bought Elizabeth Taylor. It was so large that the diamond had fallen sideways, and rested against her baby finger. She was trying to flick it straight when I opened the door. . . .

"As you can probably tell, I love this community and want to serve it," she said.

ANN BEATTIE

THE ROAD NOT TAKEN

THE ROAD NOT TAKEN

Two roads diverged in a yellow wood,
And sorry I could not travel both
And be one traveler, long I stood
And looked down one as far as I could
To where it bent in the undergrowth;

Then took the other, as just as fair,
And having perhaps the better claim,
Because it was grassy and wanted wear;
Though as for that, the passing there
Had worn them really about the same,

And both that morning equally lay
In leaves no step had trodden black.
Oh, I kept the first for another day!
Yet knowing how way leads on to way,
I doubted if I should ever come back.

I shall be telling this with a sigh
Somewhere ages and ages hence:
Two roads diverged in a wood, and I—
I took the one less traveled by,
and that has made all the difference.

ROBERT FROST

Robert Frost's poem alludes to all the important choices we make in our lives and laments that we cannot "travel both." The poem concludes that the choice the narrator makes "has made all the difference," which might be said of any and all significant choices we make. At one time or another, most of us have speculated about the roads we did not take, not necessarily in regret but perhaps in simple wonder of what might have been. If you had married that other person—the football player, the rebel, the prom queen, the Goody Two Shoes—what would your life have been like? If you had stuck with engineering instead of going into marketing, where would you be? The following exercises encourage you to incorporate these speculations into your writing, to take off on them or develop them as your whim dictates.

PANNING INSTRUCTIONS

Make a **list** of five tough choices you have faced in your life. Select one, and **freewrite** on why this was a difficult choice. Think about the option you didn't choose, and make a list tabulating the imaginary chain of consequences that might have followed if you had chosen this alternative. Draft a detailed portrait, in the third person, of the self you would be right now had you followed the alternative path. Pursue this as a poem, story, or essay, depending on where it leads you. In his poignant poem "Reunion in the Donut Shop," Bryan Pendargast imagines only a temporary reprieve from his fate and that of an old flame he runs into (see below).

EXCAVATING INSTRUCTIONS

The narrator in Frost's poem chooses to take "the road less traveled," the road that veers off the beaten path. Which of the choices you have made fall in this category? What were the least "popular" of your choices? Either as an essay, a story about a fictional character, or a poem, explore the conflicts that arise by not taking the well-worn path.

NUGGETS

REUNION IN THE DONUT SHOP

Twenty-two years. She looked her age
in the fluorescence
of Dunkin' Donuts. I could have saved her
from that. She could have saved me
from irony, her checkered-table cloth sense
of humor, a light on
in each of her eyes. So many nights

we sat above the city
in my black Mercury
we thought we were gods. We would have had

six kids and a dozen TVs, a Jesus
in every window, and for all that a short
time of it.

BRYAN PENDARGAST

ARTIFACTS

FROM THE NOVEL *IN THE NIGHT CAFE*

One morning on Seventh Street I woke up and looked around that small room. It was already getting crowded with rolled-up canvases. I stared at your brush marks on the walls. The floorboards were dappled with color; the May air smelled of turpentine. We were living inside your painting. I had a thought that took me by surprise. *I am in my life*. My real life had surrounded me. What I wanted was exactly what I had.

That was the moment, I think, when I finally gave up on the theater. It wasn't even painful. It just made sense. I saw it was what I had to do. I just decided to give you what you needed. I wanted to do it so quietly, though, you wouldn't even catch me at it.

JOYCE JOHNSON

THE BRIEFCASE

hether we carry a knapsack, pocketbook, briefcase, diaper bag, or some kind of combination of the four, many of us have trouble getting out of the house without taking some of our possessions with us. While someone totes work she hopes to do while traveling back and forth to her office, another person slips a novel into her purse in case the bus is late again. Like turtles, we tend to carry part of our world on our backs (or shoulders).

Although much of what we take with us out into the world every day is practical and necessary, hidden among the sensible calculators, notebooks, and diapers are less functional possessions, curiosities that represent the more complex realities of our daily lives.

PANNING INSTRUCTIONS

1. Empty everything out of your pocketbook, briefcase, knapsack, or baby's diaper bag on a clean surface. (This exercise works even better if you do this with a friend.) Everything. Even that moldy-looking saltine holds valuable clues. (Don't throw anything away—yet.) If you don't carry anything on a regular basis, empty your wallet of everything, even that ATM receipt you forgot to record in your checkbook.

2. Move back a few steps to gain perspective and look at all these items as someone in search of clues about your life, like an anthropologist or a detective, might look at them. Try not to judge. (All thoughts that begin with the phrase, "I can't believe I still have that stupid _____" should be immediately banished.)

Forget for the moment that these are your things, and try to imagine that they belong to someone else. What do these items tell you about this person?

(For example, several gum wrappers might suggest a nervous person; several little mirrors, a narcissistic person; several kinds of pills, a hypochondriac.) What one item among all the possessions in front of you are you most surprised to discover? (Why have you held on to that lottery ticket so long?)

3. Using these telling items as a starting point, begin a story, poem, or essay about the person whose life you have laid out before you. In the excerpt from Perri Klass's short story "A Gift of Honey Mustard" (page 120), notice how a jar of champagne honey mustard tells us a great deal about the kind of husband Alan is.

EXCAVATING INSTRUCTIONS

Look back at the item that you discovered that surprised you the most. It may be something seemingly inconsequential—someone else's business card—or seemingly more meaningful—a therapist's phone number or the wedding band you no longer wear. Often we carry things with us when we aren't sure where else to keep them or when we aren't yet ready to get rid of them. Even a dingy-looking after-dinner mint stuck to the bottom of a purse might serve to subconsciously remind someone about a much-enjoyed and long-ago night on the town.

Begin a story, poem, or essay that explores the significance of the item that most surprised you. In the excerpt from Angelin Donohue's story in progress, a single mother has to do some fast thinking to account for the toy in her purse. She doesn't yet want the man she is interested in to know that she has children (see page 120). Try completing the following sentences for triggers to get started:

1. Probably she wasn't the only person who carried a _____ (water pistol, photograph of David Bowie, and so on) with her to _____ (work, school, and so on), but she knew it wasn't likely that she'd find out who else did.

2. It didn't even mean anything to me anymore, but there it was anyway, _____ (her father's phone number, an accident lawyer's card, and so forth) accompanying me everywhere I went.

3. At first I was surprised to find _____ (his phone number, my old prescription card, and so on) in my _____, but maybe I really did intend to keep it.

 # NUGGETS

FROM A SHORT STORY IN PROGRESS

Megan hadn't meant to mislead Alan when the plastic dinosaur had fallen out of her purse. It was just that she had seen his office, with its clutter of political cartoons, his hanging rubber stork, pink slinky and other miscellaneous anti-establishment toys, and wanted him to know that she wasn't buying into the system either. So, when Alan picked it up and said "Cool," and handed the Brachiosaurus back to her with a new glimmer of recognition in his eye, she hadn't found it necessary to tell him that the toy belonged to her son, and that she had only this morning rescued it from under his car seat.

Mostly she was relieved that her purse hadn't been dumped in front of him the year before when there would have been baby wipes and a spare pacifier mixed in with the usual wallet, checkbook and keys. She decided now, today, was definitely a better time.

ANGELIN DONOHUE

 # ARTIFACTS

FROM THE SHORT STORY "A GIFT OF SWEET MUSTARD"

In his briefcase is a jar of champagne honey mustard. He has bought it partly to celebrate his own goodness as a husband; at work the blond California Girl who works in the next office had dropped in on him for a chat and suggested they go somewhere after work for a drink. Alan said he couldn't, he had to be somewhere. Of course he didn't say he had to get home to his wife, which is what a really good husband would surely have said. No one at work knows he is married. . . .

Alan is thinking about the champagne honey mustard, and how Joanna will try a little on the end of her finger and then spread it all over her share of whatever they are having for dinner.

PERRI KLASS

AROUND THE WATER COOLER

Many of us scorn gossips, imagining ourselves above listening to or spreading rumors about other people's lives. Yet, we cannot help perking up our ears when a man behind us on the bus discusses his therapy session with a friend. And not many of us can resist listening to whatever tidbit follows the phrase, "Do you promise to keep this a secret?" whether we can keep our promise or not.

Sometimes gossip is just gossip, a generally harmless distraction from our routines. But intimacies about other people's lives *can* wake us up to our own desires and fears, forcing us to question the choices we are making in our own lives. For example, while we may judge the secretary who is rumored to be sleeping with her boss, we also may be privately impressed with the risks she is taking, with how willing she seems to gain or lose so much.

PANNING INSTRUCTIONS

1. What gossip (unsubstantiated claims about events, things, or people) have you heard or helped to spread in the past year? Who told you the gossip? To help remember, think about your regular weekly routines, and make a **list** of different areas of your life in which you might hear gossip, as in the list below. If you can't remember hearing gossip in any of the places, write a question mark as shown below:

LOCATION	GOSSIP HEARD
Jake's day care	New teacher pregnant and going to quit—don't remember who said.
The carpool	??

At work | Merger? Everyone says lunch hour is going to be shortened to a half-hour.

Night school | Woman who sits next to me told me that the final exam is the same as the practice test in the back of our book.

Evie's Brownie Troop meetings | ??

2. Add to your **Gossip Heard** column by inventing likely and bizarre rumors. Be sure to incorporate any fantasies you harbor about people, as in the list below:

LOCATION	GOSSIP HEARD
Jake's day care	New teacher pregnant and going to quit—don't remember who said. **Tuition increase is really paying for teacher's *other* wardrobe in her secret life as an exotic dancer.**
The carpool	?? **Kathryn has been ten minutes late each day this week because she is secretly doing a paper route in the mornings to pay off debts.**
At work	Merger? Everyone says lunch hour is going to be shortened to a half-hour. **??**
Night school	Woman who sits next to me told me that the final exam is the same as the practice test in the back of our book. **Noisy class across the hall is really a singles' meeting and not a credit class at all.**
Evie's Brownie Troop meetings	?? **Cookies this year contain secret chemical that makes everyone feel love for their country as soon as they take a bite.**

3. Begin a story, poem, or essay that incorporates some of the "real" and invented gossip from your list. Treat all of it as fact. For an essay approach to this exercise, explain why you believe both the "real" gossip and rumors you invented to be believable.

EXCAVATING INSTRUCTIONS

What gossip might someone spread about you? What gossip would you *least* like to have spread about yourself? Go back to your list one more time and invent rumors about yourself that reflect the way you're worried others see you. Then add these new rumors to the piece you are working on. If you're writing an essay, examine your motives for inventing this gossip about yourself. Why are you afraid other people see you this way? See the examples in the **Gossip Heard** column below:

LOCATION	GOSSIP HEARD
Jake's day care	New teacher pregnant and going to quit—don't remember who said.
	Tuition increase is really paying for teacher's *other* wardrobe in her secret life as an exotic dancer.
	Teachers talk about how I'm a neglectful mother—why does he always have food stains on his face and clothes?
The carpool	??
	Kathryn has been ten minutes late each day this week because she is secretly doing a paper route in the mornings to pay off debts.
	On the Wednesdays that I'm off, they probably gossip about how run-down I'm looking, and our house is looking, lately—wonder if we're having money troubles.
At work	Merger? Everyone says lunch hour is going to be shortened to a half-hour.
	??
	Coworkers discuss the possibility of me getting fired for losing that account last month.
Night school	Woman who sits next to me told me that the final exam is the same as the practice test in the back of our book.
	Noisy class across the hall is really a singles' meeting and not a credit class at all.
	Teenagers who sit in the back gossip about my stupid middle-aged haircut.

Evie's Brownie	??
Troop meetings	Cookies this year contain secret chemical that makes everyone feel love for their country as soon as they take a bite.
	??

NUGGETS

FROM THE ESSAY "THAT'S A FACT"

Rumor has it that the stock market is going to crash. At least this is what my brother Thomas claims. He's getting a divorce or at least that's what Marcia told me. Marcia's the woman who does my nails. She does my sister-in-law's, too. Or should I say ex-sister-in-law? Not that I ever liked her that much. My brother was always a step above her on the evolution ladder. Marcia was abducted by space aliens when she was eighteen. This is, in my opinion, the one thing that makes her interesting. She showed me the exact spot she was standing in her backyard when they swooped down to get her. You don't even want to hear the details because, let me tell you, they're not very pretty. Her backyard was built over a swamp. This whole town was built on a swamp. That's why our grass is like a sponge after one brief rain shower. Don't even bother trying to find any land records to prove this. They were all burned a long time ago. In that terrible fire. The one that happened well before I got here, if you believe my Uncle Albert.

RITA MATERSON

ARTIFACTS

FROM THE SHORT STORY "GLOSSOLALIA"

Glencoe was a small town, and like all small towns it was devoted to gossip. I knew my classmates had heard about my father—many of them had probably even driven past Goodyear to see the broken window the way they'd drive past a body shop to see a car that had been totaled—but only Rob and a couple of other friends said anything. . . .

It took a couple of weeks for the gossip to reach me. One day during lunch Rob told me that Todd Knutson, whose father was a mechanic at Goodyear, was telling everybody my father had been fired for embezzling. "I know it's a dirty lie," Rob kept saying, "but some kids think he's telling the truth, so you'd better do something."

DAVID JAUSS

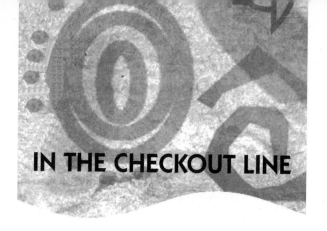

IN THE CHECKOUT LINE

Standing in a long supermarket checkout line can bring out the best and the worst in people (usually the worst). Because some people in the line are in a hurry—perhaps the dog or the baby is waiting in the car with the engine running—and because others are not in a hurry and would rather take their time sorting out their coupons, writing their checks, and then disputing the expiration date on the coupon to save a nickel on paper towels, this context is fraught with drama. Even with express lanes that limit purchases to nine or fewer items (ha!) and don't allow checks, as we all know, delays occur.

Given the emotional investment in checkout lines and the potential for conflicts, this is a context ripe for creative exploration. The following exercise asks you to invent a new approach to deal with this everyday hassle.

PANNING INSTRUCTIONS

1. Invent a **list** of items passing on the checkout conveyor belt, mixing the typical with the bizarre: a loaf of bread, a can of peaches, a divorce decree, apples, a roll of paper towels, parsley, a ringing telephone, a nightstick, a headache, a half-gallon of milk, a bag of onions, a picture of Robert Redford, Robert Redford himself. . . .

2. Linger by the checkout line and observe and jot down the bizarre or unusual combinations people really *do* purchase—for example, toilet paper, a single kiwi fruit, and a package of manila envelopes.

3. Begin a poem, story, or essay that incorporates your findings.

EXCAVATING INSTRUCTIONS

1. Write a piece that attempts to discover from the real or imagined items purchased and placed on the checkout belt what a person's life is like. Justin Cain begins to do this in "Get a Life," in which the protagonist reflects, apparently aloud, about a woman who buys a lot of cat food (see below). Allow your main character to pursue this speculation in a story, poem, or essay. Notice what purchases say about characters in John Updike's short story "A&P" (below).

2. Write a dialogue between two people in the checkout line that focuses totally on their purchases and the justification for them.

NUGGETS

FROM THE SHORT STORY "GET A LIFE"

The woman in front of me had placed maybe twenty-five cans of cat food on the conveyor belt—and for herself a carton of orange juice and a package of English muffins.

"Get a life," I heard myself saying without really wanting to say anything.

"I beg your pardon," the woman said.

I looked beyond her to the parking lot outside and said, "Oh, the kid out there on the motorcycle. I was talking to myself."

"No you weren't," she said. "You were talking to me. You think all this fuss over a cat is ridiculous, don't you?"

"Look, lady," I started to say, but then it hit me that this woman read my mind perfectly. It didn't make any sense to deny it.

JUSTIN CAIN

ARTIFACTS

FROM THE SHORT STORY "A&P"

Around they come, Queenie still leading the way, and holding a little gray jar in her hand. Slots Three through Seven are unmanned and I could see her wondering between Stokes and me, but Stokesie with his usual luck draws an old party in baggy gray pants who stumbles up with four giant cans of pineapple juice (what *do* these bums do with pineapple juice? I've often asked myself) so the girls come to me. Queenie puts down the jar and I take it into my fingers icy cold. Kingfish Fancy Herring Snacks in Pure Sour Cream: 49 cents. Now her hands are empty, not a ring or a bracelet, bare as God made them, and I wonder where the money's coming from. Still with that prim look she lifts a folded dollar bill out of the hollow at the center of her nubbled pink top. The jar went heavy in my hand. Really, I thought that was so cute.

JOHN UPDIKE

WHY I HATE VACATIONS

hile many of us may long to "get away from it all," vacations rarely completely live up to our expectations. Whether it rains the entire week we're at the beach or several colonies of ants take residence with us in the mountain cabin we have rented for a week, vacations are fraught with peril precisely because we have so much invested (emotionally and financially) in them working out well.

In addition, those vacationing together may have entirely different vacations in mind, despite the fact that they are sharing one reservation. The Yucatan Peninsula may evoke images of endless white sand beaches for one half of a couple and a week exploring Mayan ruins for the other half. A long weekend in the Amish country of Pennsylvania may send one person off daydreaming about discount outlet centers and another in search of the perfect hayride. Vacations can be relationship breakers or makers. You may feel that you never really knew someone until you spent eight solid hours in an un-airconditioned car driving through the Southwest in July with him or were stuck in a quaint but tiny room in the foot of the mountains during a three-day ice storm.

No matter how "successful" our vacations are, they are never enough. They end too soon; we come home too sunburned or were broke; and sometimes, worst of all, we return to find our old lives exactly as imperfect as we left them. Still, vacations loom large in our fantasies, and each year, despite their inevitable disappointments, we max out our credit cards and take off on them.

PANNING INSTRUCTIONS

1. Try to recall your vacation history by making a **list** of four or five vacations that you remember taking either recently or in the distant past (childhood/family vacations are often loaded with good writing material) as in the sample list below:

- The year we all went to Disneyland.
- The year mom and I went to Oregon to visit Aunt Beth. The three of us went camping.
- The summer of my first "grown-up" vacation. Went to Bermuda with Tim.
- The long weekend at the lake with Jeannie.

2. For each vacation you listed, **freewrite** on each of the following prompts for five minutes:

- Things I expected.
- Things I got.

Read over your freewriting, circling words and phrases that please you in some way.

3. Choose the vacation that you believe holds the most creative promise, and work on a poem, story, or essay that focuses on both the high and low points. If you vacationed with others, be sure to explore any tensions that developed in the relationships during the vacation.

EXCAVATING INSTRUCTIONS

Take a vacation from some aspect of your personality or behavior that you are tired of by imagining life without it. Take a break from pessimism by going to school or work without it for a day. Take a respite from your sense of responsibility by letting the kids eat dessert first. Take a vacation from your practical nature by wearing a tutu to Safeway. (Actually trying one of these things or one of the things you come up with is the best prework you can do for this exercise—except vacations from the law.) In "Dental Break," Darryl Gray fantasizes a vacation from dental chores (see below).

Write a story, poem, or essay in which you explore the ramifications of this figurative vacation. What have you gained? What have you lost? Speculate about the reactions of others to your special vacation.

NUGGETS

FROM THE ESSAY "DENTAL BREAK"

I am taking a vacation from dental responsibility. I am not brushing or flossing even though I am eating cotton candy for lunch and salt water taffy for dinner. I am letting the sugar melt in my mouth. My gums are sweet molasses. My taste buds are ringing. I am thirty-eight years old, and this is my one rebellion. I wear a coat and tie to work. My boxer shorts are clean and neatly folded. My car has air bags and anti-lock brakes. After fifteen years at the same job, I am fully vested.

At work, no one says a word, although the receptionist, a sugarless-gum snapper, seems to sniff the air a little as I walk by, a well-read copy of *Prevention* magazine in her in-box. . . .

DARRYL GRAY

 **ARTIFACTS**

FROM THE SHORT STORY "THE OCEAN"

Finding the interstate had been a problem for Bill and Imogene Crittendon. Not trusting the toll roads, they had blazed a trail to Nashville. They figured it was a three-hour drive to Nashville, but it took five, including the time they spent getting lost in the city. After driving past the tall buildings downtown and through the poor areas on the outskirts, Bill finally pulled over to the curb and Imogene said, "Hey!" to a man in a straw hat who was walking along thoughtfully. . . .

Bill had a hard time sleeping. First the dogs barked half the night. Then a man kept hollering in the distance. And at one point during the night a motorcycle came roaring into camp, setting off the dogs again. . . .

BOBBIE ANN MASON

MODERN ROMANCE

SWM 6', 38, tall, intelligent, handsome, likes long walks on the beach, love songs, birdwatching ISO S/DWF slender, 30-38, good sense of humor, looking for life partner to share joys and sorrows. Please send note and picture to . . .

Sometimes modern romance begins with the personal ads. Typically the ads describe handsome, successful people who long for romance and/or commitment. Adjectives like *dynamic, slim, humorous, warm, good looking, adventurous, youthful, sincere,* and *sensitive* abound.

It is not uncommon for ad writers to compare themselves to movie stars or even mythical figures. In a recent issue of the *Washingtonian,* an upscale magazine for those who live in the metropolitan District of Columbia area, one writer calls herself a *Katherine Hepburn type* while another describes himself as a *White Knight.*

While it makes sense that people are hesitant to admit their flaws when searching for love, it seems unlikely that this many dynamic, slim, humorous, warm, good looking, adventurous, youthful, sincere, and sensitive people even exist.

PANNING INSTRUCTIONS

1. Write a personal ad in which you describe all of your most *unattractive* qualities. Be as specific as possible and brutally honest, as Scott Patton is in "Or, You Could Bag It" (page 134). Celebrate your unique flaws and dislikes. (This ad may also be written in the form of a poem.) Some codes to help you get started:

- S = Single

- M = Married

- G = Gay
- W = White
- B = Black
- J = Jewish
- D = Divorced
- Bi = Bisexual
- ISO = In search of

2. Who would respond to your ad? Create a character who would be attracted to the "flawed" you, and have him or her write a letter back explaining why the two of you should meet for a date. Similar to the ad itself, this response may also be written in the form of a poem. For a creative nonfiction approach, describe the person you would like to answer your ad. What man or woman is worthy of falling in love with your true self?

EXCAVATING INSTRUCTIONS

Re-examine the "flaws" you describe in your personal ad and begin a poem, story, or piece of creative nonfiction defending your flaws as unique character traits. The main character in Donna Rhinegold's story (below) chews her hair, a habit her boyfriend likes. Identify several bad habits, and try answering the following questions to discover their singular value and meaning:

1. When did you begin _____ (cleaning your teeth with a credit card, chewing on your knuckle)?

2. If you stopped _____ (bouncing checks, sleeping with the TV on, and so on), would you still be you?

3. Who taught you how to _____ (slurp a soda, drink coffee out of a saucer)? What did that person mean to you?

 **NUGGETS**

A START ON A STORY

I began chewing my hair relatively late in life, during my second year in college, and I began doing it specifically when I was in doubt about the outcome of something rather imminent. I had grown increasingly doubtful about Dr. Krueshnik's ability to get through another lecture on inorganic chemistry since he appeared to have become so bored with the subject that he could hardly bring himself to pronounce the name of another reagent. This task was itself complicated by the fact that he was drunk now more often than not. Chewing the tips of my hair felt like the only thing I could do under the circumstances.

My mother noticed this habit when I came home over Christmas break, and she told me to stop many times. But I couldn't. It was so easy, my hair being right there, and there being so many things almost about to happen. Surprisingly, the boy who would become my boyfriend that year liked it that I chewed my hair. He thought it was sexy—but then he thought every nervous trait in a girl was sexy.

DONNA RHINEGOLD

 **ARTIFACTS**

FROM THE ARTICLE "OR, YOU COULD BAG IT"

. . . . I toyed briefly—about six minutes—with the idea of answering one of those personal ads in another newspaper, but I am not a "nurturing, caring, long-walks-on-the-beach, reading poetry by the fire, Alan Alda-Judd Hirsch kind of guy." Nor am I looking for someone with "plenty of love" seeking an "immediate lifetime commitment" who's "poor but rich in friends." And is anyone really looking for a "leather-loving mistress who will make you obey"? I don't think so.

Nor am I about to place such an ad: "Divorced white guy, can't dance, smokes cigars, waist size and golf handicap match, prefers long evenings in front of the TV waiting to let the dog in, not willing to drive out of N. VA., even for dinner."

SCOTT PATTON

AIR TRAVEL: UNLIKELY SEATMATES

The greatest hazard of air travel may not necessarily be a crash. Some of the people we end up sitting next to on long flights can make us wish for a fiery mid-air explosion—for example, the party treats salesman from Madison who has a theory about universal happiness or the hypochondriac who asks you to check her pulse each time the plane changes elevation or those passengers who love nothing better when they're flying than to drink—lots—and tell you very intimate things.

The following exercises draw upon your air (or bus or train) travel experiences and impressions and ask you to explore them for their creative potential.

SPANNING INSTRUCTIONS

1. Instead of people occupying seats, imagine unlikely things. For example, "On my flight to Honolulu I sat next to a gall bladder." Or, "In each seat, a different flower. I shared a chair arm with a begonia." To come up with your own unlikely items, try creating a **wordstring** using the word *airplane* as your starting point. Describe scenes in which these things make demands of flight attendants and express their own unique air travel fears—for example, "Every seat was occupied by a megaphone, and each megaphone was demanding comfort." Invent dialogues you might have with these unlikely seatmates (What do you say to a fruit basket wearing glasses and reading *Fruits* magazine?), or write about the fears and demands these things might have.

2. Recall a particularly unpleasant seatmate and describe him or her in detail. Consider using an appropriate metaphor to describe the seatmate, such as: "My seatmate was like a time bomb: everything he said sounded like it was going to go off."

3. Begin a story, poem, or essay with details you have come up with from either or both of the above activities.

EXCAVATING INSTRUCTIONS

Imagine you're in the middle of a three-seat row, and on your left and right are two old boyfriends or girlfriends—or any two people in your life who would be in conflict with each other or who both would be in conflict with you for whatever reason. Describe the flight in a poem, story, or essay. Notice how Sarah Jackson almost warms to her role as mediator between two feuding twins in the excerpt from her story "Twiddily Up and Twiddily Down" (below).

NUGGETS

FROM THE SHORT STORY "TWIDDILY UP AND TWIDDILY DOWN"

On my flight from Atlanta to Boston, I had the odd and distinct pleasure of sitting between two twins, Russ and Gus Sargeant, who were in some obscure and possibly illegal ways related to John Singer Sargeant, the great painter. They did not sit next to each other because they were having an argument, one that I think they must have had many times before, about who was born first. While there was only a matter of minutes between their births, it was very important to them who was first.

I know all this because I became the mediator in their argument. They did talk directly to each other, but they looked to me for rulings on particular points, which, being fifteen and having lived in L.A., I was both willing and qualified to make.

"I can only report what mother told me," Gus said. He was the twin who, at the beginning of the flight, sat to my right.

"That hardly qualifies," said Russ. "She told me the same thing. She told us both that we were born first."

"Ah," Gus said, "but she told me first."

"That probably doesn't mean anything," I said. This was the sort of call I would make. Often they would drag in stuff that was clearly off the point. . . .

SARAH JACKSON

■

A START FROM THE PANNING INSTRUCTIONS

On my flight to New York, I sat next to a bottle of ketchup. And across from me sat the Salt and Pepper Shakers. It wouldn't have been so bad, but the ketchup talked incessantly about how he was anticipating a speedy recovery from a broken neck. Like I could give a canary. So we talked a little, mostly he talked, and soon the Shakers were pouring out their little grains of knowledge. Pepper Shaker happened to be a podiatrist, but he had a lot of opinions about broken necks.

SEAN CARTER

 **ARTIFACTS**

FROM THE SHORT STORY "JAMIE"

The man sitting next to me on the airplane offered me his silver pouch of honey-coated peanuts. But before I could answer yes or no, he had already ripped into the pack. He was already popping nuts into his mouth. . . .

A steward brought our meal and the man next to me fidgeted in his seat. Lunch was an array of desserts: fruit cup, pudding, and date-nut bread with cream cheese. The man flashed his wallet. "Look at that angel," he said, "my baby." His baby was a four-year-old girl with a solemn smile. "The thing that kills me," the man said, "is that by the time Danielle is a woman, I'll be an old man."

I nodded and excused myself. . . .

In the airplane bathroom. I wetted my lips. My skin looked ghostly in the mirror. Every bone in my body jutted against my skin, like the girl-mummy at the Oriental Institute, delicate but gruesome. . . .

KATHLEEN MAHER

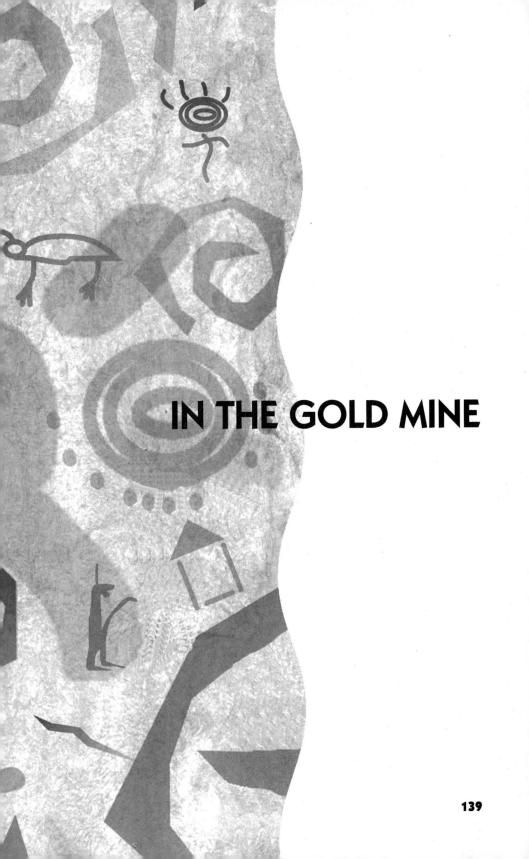

IN THE GOLD MINE

FOLK REMEDIES

olk remedies for minor maladies abound in our culture, and they are often as odd as they are colorful, combining a little science with a lot of myth. Cures for the hiccups are perhaps among the oddest and most colorful. For hiccups, we tell the victims to hold their breath and count to ten or to drink a glass of water with a spoon in it. A more radical remedy involves scaring the person half to death. And one remedy which defies reason is to twirl several strands of hair in one ear. It remains to be seen whether any of these work, though those who offer such remedies swear by them.

The following exercises ask you to try your hand at inventing "folk"-sounding remedies for the hiccups or any other minor ailment (such as itching, charley horses, yawning, sneezing, ringing in the ears, warts, acne, bunions), the odder the remedy the better. If you've inherited great folk remedies or discovered some of your own that really work, you may want to use these instead.

PANNING INSTRUCTIONS

1. Invent two plausibly odd remedies for whichever ailment you wish to cure. For the first remedy, use the prompts provided. For the second, invent your own.

- To cure _____, place two _____ in a _____ and shake. Next stand on a _____ and drink the concoction while squeezing your _____.

- To cure _____, do the following: _____.

2. Begin a poem, story, or essay that incorporates one of these "cures."

EXCAVATING INSTRUCTIONS

Problematic relationships and irritating behaviors, like hiccups and itching, have also been dealt with using folk remedies just as baffling as those for physical ailments. Folk remedies abound for repairing a broken heart: go shopping, eat chocolate, get some sleep, travel. But how do you deal with the co-worker who continually whistles "Jingle Bells" while he works, even in July? How do you handle the man who can never meet you eye-to-eye but must cast his stare south? How do you get the person who, despite your corrections, always gets your name wrong in exactly the same way—who calls you Janet when your name is Janice or Susan when your name is Suzanne?

For this exercise, develop in a poem, story, or essay a folk remedy for problematic relationships or irritating behaviors. To qualify as a folk remedy it should combine elements of common and uncommon sense. In Shirley Hickman's story "Joseph: A Man with a Mission" (below), the remedy provided by Aunt Nottie to ward off unwanted attention *almost* makes sense.

NUGGETS

FROM THE SHORT STORY "JOSEPH: A MAN WITH A MISSION"

According to my Aunt Nottie, if you wanted to get a man to stop looking at you, one sure way of doing it was to complain about your teeth. This, of course, would probably not work with a dentist, but then Joseph was not a dentist. So following her advice, I let it be known in the loudest way that my teeth were like toppling, unvisited gravestones.

In the break room one afternoon, there I was and there Joseph was, staring, ogling, preparing to begin to start to say something he concluded after long thought was clever but which would undoubtedly be insulting or just stupid. I bought a Snickers candy bar, took one bite and let out a shriek that probably woke up half the employees on the graveyard shift. Joseph looked genuinely startled.

"What's wrong?" he asked.

I palmed my jaw, winced and mumbled as though through swollen cheeks, "My tooth. I think I broke another one."

"Another one?"

"Yep, I don't have but maybe two good teeth in this head."

And then, wouldn't you know it, the fool smiled.

"And such a pretty head it is," he said.

I don't think my Aunt Nottie's wisdom grew out of a world with dental plans. Joseph seemed like a man prepared to see me through every root canal and bridge any dentist could build in my mouth. I needed another strategy.

Shirley Hickman

From a start on a short story "One Idea"

"To cure athlete's foot, place two pennies in a vodka tonic and shake. Next, stand on a catamaran and drink the concoction while squeezing your ankle."

This is the advice that my uncle gave me when I was twelve. I had never had athlete's foot before, but I hoped there was some other way to get rid of it. For one thing, I wasn't allowed to drink yet and for another, no one I knew had a catamaran. My uncle had a row boat that he called his yacht. He kept it in our backyard, and I don't know when the last time he took it out was. It was filled with rain water and leaves, which maybe was a good sign: if the rain didn't leak out there couldn't have been any holes in it. Not that I could ever imagine him actually carrying that boat down to the river that ran just outside of town. My uncle was more of a talker than a doer. . . .

Sean Carter

 **ARTIFACTS**

How to Cure Your Fever

Pull your bed aside and dig
a hole in the dirt floor.

Trick your wife, the one you divorced
a hundred years ago, so that
she falls asleep in this hole.

Replace as much dirt as possible.

Now drag the bed back
and center it over the spot.

As your fever subsides
think of the lawnmower in your heart,
try not to freeze.

THOMAS LUX

THE CLICHÉ'S THE THING

I t was a decent living. Even though I worked like a dog with my nose to the grindstone, I ate three square meals a day. Anyway, complaining wouldn't get me anywhere. I got up when the rooster crowed at the crack of dawn and went to bed when night fell. Weekends, I'd paint the town red. Sundays I'd put on my Sunday-go-to-meeting clothes and go to church . . .

If this passage fails to rivet your attention, it might be because it is full of phrases so familiar and overused that you no longer even hear them. At one time, perhaps the expression "three square meals a day" seemed like a clever and snappy thing to say. Likewise, "nose to the grindstone" once probably evinced winces with its painful imagery. But because we've heard these expressions so often, we no longer really visualize the imagery they create. When a word, phrase, or gesture reaches this degree of familiarity, it's called a cliché.

If the creative can be characterized as fresh, surprising, and original, then clichés, in any realm—words, ideas, gestures—might be considered the opposite: stale, predictable, stock. Clichés have their place in our conversations, but in creative writing, resorting to them can deaden or obscure the fresh things we're trying to say and give the impression of imaginative laziness.

Still, few writers can totally avoid clichés because clichés do have the power of lived truths, however familiar their expressions. An excellent and fun way of training the mind and ear to detect clichés is to embrace them and try to recast them in new ways and contexts—and in the process perhaps to discover some ideas for beginning poems, stories, or essays.

PANNING INSTRUCTIONS

List as many clichés as you can. Mix and match key parts of several different clichés and try to come up with expressions that sound like clichés but are, in fact, new, as the late Weldon Kees does in the poem "Back" (page 147). Mixing and matching some of the clichés from the example given at the beginning of this exercise might result in something like the following:

> I worked like a decent rooster.
>
> Crowing wouldn't get me to Sunday.
>
> I went to bed when night cracked.
>
> I ate the red grindstone and painted three square dogs a day.

While largely nonsense, the above passage nevertheless sounds familiar, which makes the reader work for the sense it does make. In this way, modified clichés can forcefully direct the reader's attention.

Try your hand at writing a few lines of poetry or prose that use modified clichés. If you have trouble coming up with clichés—which, with respect to creative writing, would be a "good" failure—choose a few from the following list:

as old as the hills	a tower of strength
as a crow flies	proud as a peacock
one thing or another	like a house on fire
to beat the band	sharp as a tack
the whole nine yards	smart as a whip
lock, stock, and barrel	gentle as a lamb
everything but the kitchen sink	hard as a rock
till hell freezes over	dead as a doornail
fair to middlin'	true to life
nine-to-five job	easy as pie
almighty dollar	as a matter of fact
there but for the grace of God	fair but firm
excuse me for living	bigger than life
federal case	around the clock
to tell the truth	a coon's age
kicked the bucket	rock bottom
hightailed it out of here	a slow death
the bottom line	raining cats and dogs

EXCAVATING INSTRUCTIONS

Write a poem, story, or essay that literalizes, engages, or challenges the truth expressed in a cliché.

To literalize a cliché, you simply take an expression, like "kicked the bucket," which means to die, and make it actual or real—for example, "Yesterday, my dad kicked the bucket. He kicked it down the stairs. Kicked it into the yard. He was so angry, he kicked it into Mr. Simmon's ornamental cabbage garden. . . ."

To engage a cliché is to illustrate and use its truth. For example, "When my brother disputed his tax bill, he was in fact making a federal case out of it. He had no choice. And a federal case is different from other kinds of cases in ways that astonish even attorneys."

To challenge a cliché is to refute the common truth associated with it. For example, "No nine-to-five job is ever just nine-to-five . . . usually they're more like 7:30 to 6:30 by the time you add in driving and overtime . . . and that's my problem with the expression."

 **NUGGETS**

PIETY

Pull the wolf over her eyes:
Darkness is a trick
to a woman sacrificed.

Moss grows thick
on word and heart,
hiding forests from trees,

shading dawn from the sun.
Still, the Wolf of God
watches as she bleeds,

grins as she squints
through the hood
toward the moonlight.

He wants to crack her bones,
but his own skeleton
still isn't dry.

Pull the wolf over her eyes;
darkness is a trick
to a woman sacrificed.

PEGGY BAIR

ARTIFACTS

BACK

Much cry and little wool
I have come back
As empty-handed as I went.

Although the woods are full,
And past the track
The heavy boughs are bent

Down to my knees with fruit
Ripe for a still life, I had meant
My trip as a search for stones.

But the beach was bare
Except for drying bones
Of a fish, shells, an old wool

Shirt, a rubber boot,
A strip of lemon rind.
They were not what I had in mind.

It was merely stones.
Well, the days are full.
This day at least is spent.

Much cry and little wool:
I have come back
As empty-handed as I went.

WELDON KEES

MIXING RELATIONSHIP BOUNDARIES

To identify a relationship is, to a certain degree, to circumscribe it. Friends, lovers, spouses, parents, children, brothers, sisters—all name relationships that have as many limits as rewards. We do things with our children we would not ordinarily do with our spouses or siblings, and vice versa. You might say that your father is your best friend, but would this really be a good relationship if it were true? We instinctively scrutinize mother/daughter relationships that get too much like friendships—the mother who flirts with her daughter's friends or who dresses a generation away from her own closet.

However, within limits, it might be said that the best relationships of any kind are those that threaten to cross boundaries, while nevertheless resisting for the good of all. The following assignment is designed to explore the boundaries of relationships and to play with them creatively.

PANNING INSTRUCTIONS

Make up several **lists** that complete the following statement for different relationships:

Things I Do with My (Fill In A Relationship) that I Would Never Do with My (Fill In A Relationship).

Example: Things I Do with My *Sister* that I Would Never Do with My *Best Friend*.

* Share shoes

* Hit each other over the head

* Lip sync to songs on the radio

Next, begin a poem, story, or essay in which you do some of the things that you say you would never do. In the beginning of an essay by Mark Lovell (below), a father reflects on an odd development in his relationship with his eight-year-old son.

EXCAVATING INSTRUCTIONS

Create or describe a relationship between two people in the act of redefining the boundaries of their relationship. For an example, see the excerpt from *A Home at the End of the World* (below), where a mother smokes marijuana with her son and her son's friend. In Theodore Roethke's classic poem "Elegy for Jane" (page 150), a teacher questions his "right" to feel certain emotions about a student.

NUGGETS

A BEGINNING OF AN ESSAY

I don't know when I started asking my son for advice. Sometimes it seems like decades ago, but I know that can't be right: he's only eight. . . . I seem to recall him telling me we should just go ahead and buy a new car after I'd complained to him about the difficulty of making payments on my salary. "Get a second job at night," he advised. Was he only five then?

MARK LOVELL

ARTIFACTS

FROM THE NOVEL *A HOME AT THE END OF THE WORLD*

As I put the cigarette to my lips, I was aware of myself standing in a pale blue blouse and wraparound skirt in my son's bedroom, about to perform the first plainly illegal act of my life. I inhaled. The smoke was so harsh and bitter I nearly choked. My eyes teared, and I could not hold the smoke in my lungs as Bobby had told me to do. I immediately blew out a thick cloud that hung in the air, raggedly intact, for a full second before dissipating.

Nevertheless, the boys cheered. I handed the cigarette to Bobby.

"You did it," he said. "You did it."

MICHAEL CUNNINGHAM

FROM THE POEM "ELEGY FOR JANE"

My Student, Thrown by a Horse

If only I could nudge you from this sleep,
My maimed darling, my skittery pigeon.
Over this damp grave I speak the words of my love:
I, with no rights in this matter,
Neither father nor lover.

THEODORE ROETHKE

WHAT THINGS SAY

Writing teachers often enjoin their students to "show, not tell," and in so doing they emphasize the imagination's dependence on and delight in words that appeal to the senses—or images. It isn't that words that characterize or summarize or generalize—words like *hate, love, ugly, smart, sad, stupid, playful, dangerous, horrible, good,* or *bad*— are in any absolute sense bad. Such words have their place. But often they simply aren't enough to convey a unique idea, or, at their worst, they tell the reader how to feel without giving her a chance to form her own impressions from events and other details.

Consider the following two statements about the same character:

1. The waiter left the check, and Harold calculated the tip based on a straight 15 percent, which came to $1.90. He called the waiter back and asked for change for a dollar, and he left all but the dime on the other dollar bill. He placed the dime in his change purse, a shiny red plastic device that opened like a wound.

2. Harold was cheap.

As a reader you may or may not agree with the wholesale conclusion that Harold was cheap, but we suspect that most readers would come away with something more from the first passage. Usually, readers would rather use their imaginations to discern the meanings of concrete details than to be told what things mean at the outset. When writers force their judgments, conclusions, or generalizations on readers without providing the details, the readers lose patience, as well they should.

PANNING INSTRUCTIONS

1. Try your hand at replacing the following wholesale judgments with your own specific details (using words that appeal directly to the senses):

- She was an awkward conversationalist.

- The room smelled funny.

- He was a bad father.

- His car was a real jalopy.

2.   Begin a story, poem, or essay that incorporates one of your developed descriptions.

EXCAVATING INSTRUCTIONS

Because everyone is unique and because no one can know for sure what's going through another person's mind, people are by their very nature mysterious. Often people don't even know themselves well enough to describe their own characters; so whether it's healthy or not, we often look for and rely on clues about each other in trying to infer each other's needs, desires, and motives. It's as though we're all low-level sleuths: we observe how a friend suddenly turns down an offer of a beer or how our boss begins to close his door after years of leaving it open, and we wonder what it all means. What can we infer from these details?

In a fashion similar to Weldon Kees's poem "Crime Club" (page 153), begin a story, essay, or poem by describing objects in a room that both raise questions about the inhabitant and also provide some answers. Notice how Jonathan Francis concludes from his prospective dorm mate's possessions that his father followed him to college (below).

NUGGETS

FROM THE ESSAY "MY NEW ROOMMATE"

I had hoped to check into my dorm room before my assigned dorm mate, whoever that might be, so that I could tag the best bed. But I was too late. He had already been there. Moreover, judging from the objects my new roommate dumped in the room, whether or not I got the best bed would be the least of my worries. An issue of *Golf Life*? A rotary rack of tobacco pipes? A suitcase of unopened scotch and vodka bottles? Suddenly, I thought my dad had followed me to college and decided to move in with me. . . .

JONATHAN FRANCIS

ARTIFACTS

CRIME CLUB

No butler, no second maid, no blood upon the stair.
No eccentric aunt, no gardener, no family friend
Smiling among the bric-a-brac and murder.
Only a suburban house with the front door open
And a dog barking at a squirrel, and the cars
Passing. The corpse quite dead. The wife in Florida.

Consider the clues: the potato masher in a vase,
The torn photograph of a Wesleyan basketball team,
Scattered with check stubs in the hall;
The unsent fan letter to Shirley Temple,
The Hoover button on the lapel of the deceased,
The note: "To be killed this way is quite all right with me."

Small wonder that the case remains unsolved,
Or that the sleuth, Le Roux, is now incurably insane,
And sits alone in a white room in a white gown,
Screaming that all the world is mad, that clues
lead nowhere, or to walls so high their tops cannot be seen;
Screaming all day of war, screaming that nothing can be
solved.

WELDON KEES

CHANGES IN PREFERENCE

Most of us are creatures of habit. This is particularly true with matters of taste. Some people would rather reverse their positions on capital punishment than reconsider their opinion of liverwurst. For every thousand people who change their party affiliations from Republican to Democrat, perhaps two will decide to give opera another chance. Significant change is inherently telling and dramatic.

The following exercises ask you to explore changes in preferences as potential sources of ideas for stories, poems, or essays. As you have been doing with the other exercises in this book, jump into these exercises uncritically and see where they take you. They may lead you into a scene or a character portrait or an entire short story—or you might discover some ideas better developed in an essay format.

PANNING INSTRUCTIONS

Consider the history of one or two of your own preferences, and **freewrite** on the process you went through in establishing the preference, as nearly as you can remember. In this account, address some or all of the following questions:

- When did you start liking or hating some of the things you now like or hate?

- What was going on when you developed these preferences?

- Who was involved?

- Was there one incident that shaped your desire?

 EXCAVATING INSTRUCTIONS

Try accounting for one of your own changes of preference or inventing a situation that gives rise to a change of preference in a fictional character. Such changes are not always rational and well-thought-out. As with the poem "A Bird a Boy and His Cups" (below), such changes sometimes appear to come from nowhere or from events that seem to have no relationship to the change.

NUGGETS

A Bird a Boy and His Cups

All afternoon I watched my son discover
and rediscover his red, blue
and yellow cups, each
a different size. It would be a month
before he stacked them right. For now
they were hard and bright
and they held each other sometimes.

On the deck rail a large starling
also watched. The bird cocked its head
approvingly, I would say, and seemed to reach
some judgments about the boy's promise.

Suddenly, I wanted to eat a fresh
lemon, a fruit whose flavor, I swear
to you, I never liked and have since
never ceased to like. If I were called

before the court of tongues
as a witness, I would still have little
to say for the lemon, only
that it is yellow and sour,
sometimes surprising,
but mainly yellow and sour.

Frank Slavinski

 # ARTIFACTS

FROM THE SHORT STORY "JUGGLING"

Wayne says of all the players involved, why should Joanne be the one Tyler blames. He says Tyler has to learn to look inside himself for answers and not to the outside world for fault. At Julia's house, Tyler's father made herb tea and asked Tyler to have a seat. Julia's at her aerobics class, Calvin said, otherwise she would be happy to meet you. Tyler had never seen his father drink anything warm. In the mornings he drank orange juice but never coffee. At night ice floated in his drinks.

SUZANNE GREENBERG

SUBTITLES AND DOUBLETALK

Sometimes what we say to people is not exactly what we mean—or *all* that we mean. We may politely tell a telemarketer trying to sell us credit card protection or vacation condos, "Thanks, but I'm not interested," when our actual thoughts say, "You total idiot! I'm so sick of these calls! Go jump in a lake." And when someone you really don't want to see, much less talk to, wants to get together for lunch, manners dictate that you uplift even as you let down by saying something like, "What a great idea. Maybe next week when things slow down at work a bit," while your thoughts are saying, "Give up a lunch hour to someone who never stops talking about herself? No way!"

These exercises ask you to take a closer look at conversations you have had in which you have sacrificed honesty for politeness or simply tried too hard to be "nice."

PANNING INSTRUCTIONS

Recall a situation where you said one thing to someone—for example, your boss, a relative, or a friend—but felt or thought something entirely different. **Freewrite** about this for awhile, recording what you said and thought and exploring why you didn't say what you thought. Next, write a segment of dialogue in which you include what you said as best as you can recall; then write what you were actually thinking in parentheses. (This may sound challenging, but in virtually every conversation we have we leave out things or say things dictated by manners.) The following is an example of one student's dialogue:

Mother: Honey, I've got something important to tell you.

Daughter: Oh, yeah? (Oh, no. This doesn't sound good.)

Mother:	Chuck and I have finally decided to make it official.
Daughter:	Official? (Oh, God, I hope this isn't what it sounds like.)
Mother:	That's right. We're getting married. Tying the knot.
Daughter:	That's terrific, Mom. I'm so happy for you. (When can I throw up? I hope you don't expect me to participate in this farce.)
Mother:	And guess who I want to be my bridesmaid? What do you think, honey? I'd be so proud.
Daughter:	Of course, Mom. Thanks for asking me. (Thanks for putting me on the spot here. You just knew I couldn't say no.)
Mother:	Oh, I'm so excited. I know I must sound like a silly teenager, but I swear, honey, I feel like I'm eighteen all over again.
Daughter:	You don't sound silly at all. You just sound happy. (You sound like an idiot. Why does getting married reduce women's IQs this way?)

EXCAVATING INSTRUCTIONS

Write a scene in which one of the speakers once again says one thing but means another. This time allow your narration (the non-dialogue part) to reveal the character's true feelings. You may wish to develop the scene you created for the Panning Instructions (as in "My Mother's Marriage" by Irene Cabel, below) or to invent an entirely new scene.

If you're working on an essay, recall a time when your words were less than honest. If you're working on fiction or poetry, invent a character and a scene or change the facts of something that really happened.

NUGGETS

FROM THE ESSAY "MY MOTHER'S MARRIAGE"

When my mother called to tell me that she was marrying Chuck, I said, "That's terrific, Mom. I'm so happy for you," although the truth was I didn't exactly feel like celebrating. My mother had been dating Chuck, a man who insisted on calling me "Renie" even though no one else did, and I hated it, for five years so it was hardly a surprise. Still, this was mother we were talking about, the woman who had married my father once upon a time and who now was planning to marry a man who made Andy Griffith seem like a big-city sophisticate.

"And guess who I want to be my bridesmaid?" she said next. "What do you think, honey? I'd be so proud."

I could just see her examining her manicure at the other end of the line while she waited for me to answer. My mother was small and Southern and always well-groomed. Me, I was five-foot-ten by the time I was fourteen and had to buy my size-eleven shoes from a catalog if I wanted any kind of selection. The only thing we had in common was my dad, who gave her me, gave me my ungainly size, and then left us both. Still, she was my mother and I felt I had an obligation not to ruin her happiness.

"Of course, Mom. Thanks for asking me," was all I said. . . .

Irene Cabel

 **ARTIFACTS**

From the short story "A Good Bet"

Ada picks up the phone when Phil calls to check in. She would like to tell him the truth, that his daughter is sullen and lacks the ability to concentrate. But Phil already has enough problems. "We went to the movies tonight," Ada lies. "Something with John Wayne in it. Something about the west."

This seems to satisfy Phil. Ada can tell because he is quiet after she says it.

"She's a good girl," Ada says.

"That's good," Phil says. "John Wayne is good."

When Phil hangs up, Ada is alone with her heart again. But her heart is quiet. She takes the stethoscope that she stole from her doctor out of her night drawer and listens to the pounding, the everydayness of it, until she falls asleep.

Suzanne Greenberg

"THE MARIGOLD IS LIKE A STALLED SCHOOL BUS"

Whether a story, poem, or essay seems to "flow" right out of our pens or stubbornly demands that we fight for each word, as writers we are always making choices. Often these choices are made so quickly, we don't realize we're even making them. For example, a writer may begin an autobiographical piece with the sentence "I grew up in Omaha," which seems to him a logical, straight-forward enough place to start. But even in this simple sentence, he has made several choices. For example, in writing that he "grew up," we know that he now considers himself "grown up" (whatever that may mean) and that he will be writing from a certain distance. If, however, he wrote that he "was raised," the tone would be slightly different. We might be expecting parents or guardians to show up in the piece fairly soon, and we might not be sure if the writer has completely "grown up" yet. In writing that he "grew up in Omaha," the writer is letting us know that he identifies clearly with this city, and perhaps to a lesser degree with the entire state of Nebraska.

"Who reads this way?" you might be wondering. And, of course, most readers aren't calculated dissectors; it's much more likely that they're simply reading for enjoyment. But readers do make these kinds of inferences and judgments in a much quieter, more subconscious way, the same way we make many of our decisions as writers.

In this exercise, you'll look more closely at some of the automatic choices you make as you write and explore less predictable choices.

PANNING INSTRUCTIONS

Writing about flowers tends to compel many of us to use very predictable language—pretty, delicate, sweet, and so on. In this exercise, pick the flower of your choice to describe in a new, unexpected way.

Following the examples below, describe your flower using each of the parts of speech listed:

Verbs

The marigolds *explode*.
The _____ _____.
     your flower   your verb

Adjectives

The *depressed* marigolds explode.
The _____ _____ _____.
  your adjective your flower   your verb

Adverbs

The marigolds explode *gratefully*.
The _____ _____ _____.
  your flower   your verb   your adverb

Similes

The marigold is like *a stalled school bus*.
The _____ is like _____.
  your flower   your simile

Metaphors

The rusted yellow marigold is *the hubcap of innocence*.
The _____ is _____.
  your flower your metaphor

Repetition

Marigold, marigold, my arrogance for a *marigold*.
_____.
      your choices

Word play order

Gratefully explode the marigolds on the porch.
_____.
      your choices

Word arrangement

Gratefully   the mari
EXPLODE   golds
   On The Porch

(your choices)

2. Begin a poem, story, or essay that incorporates one or more of the discoveries you have made taking your flower through the exercise above. Notice the way Theodore Roethke in his poem "The Geranium" compares a geranium to a dog at one point, as well as the surprising verb he uses in the last line of this first stanza (page 163).

Instead of choosing a flower, choose or create a person and revisit the list above, filling in the blanks this time with unpredictable descriptions of this person, as in the samples using "son" below:

Verb   My son *ignites*.

Adjective   My *disgraced* son ignites.

Use some or all of your findings as the basis for a poem, story, or essay. Notice the unusual simile Pete Garrison creates about the baby-sitter in his story "Locked Out" (below).

NUGGETS

FROM THE STORY "LOCKED OUT"

"Let me in!" Jennifer shrieked.

Dave smiled and stuck three more of the Lifesavers he had taken from her purse in his mouth. Jennifer was his babysitter, and he had locked her out on the deck. Dave planned to let her back in but not until she had paid for hiding the remote control so they wouldn't have to watch *Aladdin* again, even though he had only seen it one-and-a-half times this particular Saturday afternoon. Not until she paid for telling him that if he got some fresh air, maybe he wouldn't be so fat.

Jennifer was like a too bright Monday morning all weekend long, and Dave should know, stuck as he was with her every weekend all spring since his mother had become a realtor. . . .

PETE GARRISON

 **ARTIFACTS**

From the poem "The Geranium"

When I put her out, once, by the garbage pail,
She looked so limp and bedraggled,
So foolish and trusting, like a sick poodle,
Or a wizened aster in late September,
I brought her back in again
For a new routine—
Vitamins, water, and whatever
Sustenance seemed sensible
At the time: she lived
So long on gin, bobbie pins, half-smoked cigars, dead beer,
Her shriveled petals falling
On the faded carpet, the stale
Steak grease stuck to her fuzzy leaves.
(Dried-out, she creaked like a tulip.)

Theodore Roethke

MORPHEMES

P ity this busy monster, manunkind,
  not. Progress is a comfortable disease:

FROM "PITY THIS BUSY MONSTER, MANUNKIND," BY E. E. CUMMINGS

Many words we use are themselves composed of smaller units of meaning (called morphemes), whether prefixes or suffixes, in addition to the root words. For example, the word *unrewarding* can be broken up into four distinct units of meaning: *un,* meaning "not"; *re,* meaning "anew or again"; the root word *ward,* in this case meaning "to be watched, taken care of"; and *ing,* meaning "action or process." Adding these meanings together in a loose literal fashion, we arrive at an almost foreign-sounding expression: the "not be cared for anew process."

As foreign as this expression may sound, it also has poetic potential, as the following student example illustrates:

Un-
Rewarding

There are ways
I will not care

anew . . . this is one:

I will flatten my face
against the lake's surface
as though it were a window
I could breathe and call
your name. Un-

rewarding is what you'll say
about my love.

Breaking familiar words open like this can create a refreshing strangeness as well as provide some ideas for stories, essays, and poems. Notice the way the examples by e. e. cummings change our appreciation of the familiar words *trespass* (see page 167) and *mankind* (in the epigram on page 164) by breaking the former down and by appending the latter with an unusual prefix (*manunkind*).

PANNING INSTRUCTIONS

Choose one of the following polymorphic words (or choose one of your own); break it down into its prefixes, suffixes, and root (you'll need a good hardbound dictionary); and begin a poem, story, or essay using liberal translations of the literal meanings.

- unexcited
- antipathy
- disingenuously
- professionally
- procrastinating
- reproduction
- despicable
- disreputable
- delightful

EXCAVATING INSTRUCTIONS

Choose a root word (one that has only one morpheme—for example, *grace, slice, judge*) and add your own prefixes and suffixes to create new words, as is illustrated below with the word *grace*:

- gracely
- regracing
- graceable

- pregrace

- postgrace

- graceness

Create your own definition of one of these and use your definition to begin a story, poem, or essay.

 **NUGGETS**

Delightful

de - to undo, away from, off, down, wholly, entirely
light - to come to rest after traveling through air
ful - containing a particular quality or characteristic, apt

Fill
Your self
With heed
Oh, my heart
  For you
(Like chianti
  splashed
  against
  a fan)
are wholly
  apt
to come
to rest
after traveling
  through
the air

Sean Carter

From the story "Martha's Vinegar"

"Graceable" is my term for the ability to attain social competence, and in my view Martha was not graceable. Her ingraceability owed largely to her belief that she was a descendant of Cleopatra. You would think that grace would attend this fantasy the way rain attends clouds, but no.

Martha's Cleopatra stumbled on her jeweled sandals, strangled herself on her own necklaces and offended those she most wanted to amuse.

ALISON LIGHTFOOT

 **ARTIFACTS**

OLD AGE STICKS

old age sticks
up Keep
Off
signs)&

youth yanks them
down(old
age cries No

Tres)&(pas)
youth laughs
(sing
old age

scolds Forbid
den Stop
Must
n't Don't

&)youth goes
right on
gr
owing old

E. E. CUMMINGS

CREATING THE EVIL TWIN

Throughout literature, there are countless examples of character opposites, from Cain and Abel to Dr. Jekyll and Mr. Hyde. In fact, many psychologists assert that within each of us our opposite lurks. Our opposite cheats on his spouse while we remain faithful, spends the night dancing while we sit at home studying, curses at the boss while we smile and hold our tongue.

Our opposite self, or alter ego, isn't always *worse* in some way than we are; in fact, our "evil twin" is generally accomplished at the very things we think we are failures at. If you are shy, he is a grandiose flirt. If you oversleep, he is up each day to watch the sunrise. If you are afraid of flying, he has acquired enough frequent-flyer miles to circle the globe twice.

Many writers find it creatively liberating to give expression to that shadow figure who lives the life we only dream of living. The following exercises give you the license to indulge "the other."

PANNING INSTRUCTIONS

1. Complete the following statements about yourself, or, if you would rather create a character, complete these statements about the character you have invented. (Feel free to add new descriptive statements as they occur to you):

- I am a (circle one) *night, morning* person.

- I am happiest when my life is (circle one) *settled, swirling*.

- My favorite kind of music is _____.

- I would describe my style of clothes as _____.

- My idea of a perfect evening is _____.

- My idea of a perfect job is _____.

- If I found a wounded sparrow I would _____.

- The best place in the world to live is _____.

- If I found a wallet with money in it, I would _____.

- My relationship with my parents is/was _____.

2. Now complete the same statements in their opposite way. For the first two, simply pick the adjective you didn't pick the first time. For the others, come up with what you consider to be the opposite description. For example, one person whose favorite kind of music is *rap* might say that the opposite of rap is *bluegrass* while another person who chose rap for her favorite kind of music might say that *classical* is rap's natural opposite. There are no right or wrong answers here; what's important is that *you* see two things as being diametrically opposed to each other (opposite):

- I am a (circle one) *night, morning* person.

- I am happiest when my life is (circle one) *settled, swirling.*

- My favorite kind of music is _____.

- I would describe my style of clothes as _____.

- My idea of a perfect evening is _____.

- My idea of a perfect job is _____.

- If I found a wounded sparrow I would _____.

- The best place in the world to live is _____.

- If I found a wallet with money in it, I would _____.

- My relationship with my parents is/was _____.

3. Begin a story, poem, or essay in which the character you created finds herself living in a way that includes more of the details from the *second* list than from the first and is therefore living in a way that is antithetical to her personality. For example, a character whose idea of a perfect job is sitting in a quiet office editing copy might find herself taking a group of screaming three-year-olds on a field trip to see the Liberty Bell. Or a character who couldn't imagine ever living anywhere but New York City might find herself in a small town in Tennessee. If you are working on an essay, think of a time when you found some essential part of yourself at odds with your environment or circumstances.

For an example of a fictional approach to this exercise, notice the way the young Jing-Mei Woo, in the excerpt from *The Joy Luck Club*, resists her mother's attempts to turn her into the child prodigy she knows that she isn't (see page 171).

EXCAVATING INSTRUCTIONS

Look over your two lists again. This time create two characters from these lists who end up meeting and in some way affecting each other's lives. While the cliché that "opposites attract" is rarely true, those who seem to be our opposite can make strong and lasting impressions as they force us to examine our own personalities, predilections, and, possibly, lost opportunities.

Notice the way the narrator in Linda Shear's "Laura Ashley of Hollywood" (below) immediately dislikes her *apparent* opposite, but they soon seem to find a rhythm of relating to each other. And in the essay "My Brother, My Self," the differences between himself and his brother cause the writer, Dick Schaap, to examine his own choices (see page 172).

NUGGETS

FROM THE ESSAY "LAURA ASHLEY OF HOLLYWOOD"

I disliked Toni immediately and couldn't imagine who wouldn't. She wore earrings that were too large, a shirt and jeans that were too tight and a fragrance that smelled like overripe bananas. My own tastes were more Laura Ashley than Fredericks of Hollywood, but here we were, forced by an overcrowded bus, to be sitting next to each other for a four-hour trip. I opened my book and prepared to settle in to a murder mystery that I had coveted for just this opportunity.

"Say, what are you reading?" she said.

"It's a mystery," I told her without looking up, hoping she would get the hint.

"Boring," she said. "I can already tell you what happened. Someone died and someone killed him. Ha! Give me a good romance anyday."

"A romance?" I said. "I can already tell you what happened. Someone fell in love and someone got hurt."

"Ha! Got me on that one," she said.

I put my book away and decided to give her a chance. . . .

LINDA SHEAR

ARTIFACTS

FROM THE NOVEL *THE JOY LUCK CLUB*

My mother believed you could be anything you wanted to be in America. You could open a restaurant. You could work for the government and get good retirement. You could buy a house with almost no money down. You could become rich. You could become instantly famous.

"Of course you can be prodigy, too," my mother told me when I was nine. . . .

In fact, in the beginning, I was just as excited as my mother, maybe even more so. I pictured this prodigy part of me as many different images, trying each one on for size. I was a dainty ballerina girl standing by the curtains, waiting to hear the right music that would send me floating on my tiptoes. I was like the Christ-child lifted out of the straw manger, crying with holy indignity. I was Cinderella stepping from her pumpkin carriage with sparkly cartoon music filling the air. . . .

"You want me to be someone that I'm not!" I sobbed. "I'll never be the kind of daughter you want me to be!"

"Only two kinds of daughters," she shouted in Chinese. "Those who are obedient and those who follow their own mind! Only one kind of daughter can live in this house. Obedient daughter!"

"Then I wish I wasn't your daughter. I wish you weren't my mother," I shouted. As I said these things I got scared. I felt like worms and toads and slimy things were crawling out of my chest, but it also felt good *as if this awful side of me had surfaced, at last* [emphasis added].

AMY TAN

From the essay "My Brother, My Self"

I do not really know my brother. I do not see him often or speak to him regularly, even though we live in the same city and we both make our living with words. We both consider ourselves to be, above all else, journalists, and yet, professionally, our paths almost never cross, and we rarely turn to each other for either advice or criticism. We are not close, not in any customary sense of the word, and yet I love him very much and admire him immensely. . . . I think it is because he is the me I once wanted to be, the me I might have been, the me I'll never be.

I work for ABC. My brother works against the CIA. I write, mostly, to entertain, to make people smile, perhaps even laugh. My brother writes, mostly, to incite, to make people angry, perhaps even act. I am a correspondent for ABC News, specializing, until recently, in sports. My brother is one of the three editors of the *Covert Action Information Bulletin*. I cover the American League. He covers American imperialism. I go to the Super Bowl and the Boston Marathon. He goes to Cuba and Nicaragua. . . .

I am what is called, not always with a scorn, a television personality. My brother is a radical, a full-time, grown-up radical, a rare breed, a writer and an editor and a publisher. People who watch me on television, and see him in print, know that we are very different. We always were. . . .

Dick Schaap

CHARACTER BY ASSOCIATION

W hen describing people, many of us look for the one perfect word that says it all. "The problem with my roommate is he's a real *neat freak*." "My first wife was a total *bookworm*." But while it can be satisfying to sum up others this way, these brief descriptions are almost always too limited to do complex beings justice. While a *neat freak* may spend an excessive amount of time straightening up and a *bookworm* an unusual amount of time reading, certainly these descriptions do not take into account their entire characters.

In the following exercise, we ask you to explore new ways of discovering and describing character that should encourage you to look at real and/or fictional people in a way that does justice to the complexity of humankind.

PANNING INSTRUCTIONS

1. Think about a person you know fairly well—a friend, relative, or coworker —that you would like to write about for whatever reason. Then answer the following questions with respect to this person. Or, begin to invent a character by answering the following questions:

If this person were a _____, what _____ would he or she be?

- Animal _____
- Flower _____
- Tree _____
- Color _____
- Food _____

- Country _____
- Model of car _____
- Kitchen utensil _____
- Odor _____
- Playing card _____
- Month _____
- Radio station _____
- Body of water _____
- Brand of soap _____
- Piece of jewelry _____

2.   Begin a story, poem, or essay that incorporates one or more of the connections you have made above. Notice the way Judy Grahn compares Ella to a copperhead snake and later to an "isolated lake" in her poem "Ella, in a square apron, along Highway 80" (page 175). We included three associations that Kevin Harris used to develop "Howard" (see below). The animal that came to mind when Kevin thought about Howard was a giraffe, which suggested risk taking. To others, a giraffe might suggest gentleness.

EXCAVATING INSTRUCTIONS

Instead of describing your character *as* one or more of the items listed above, link him or her to one of the things or places you have listed in a way that *indirectly* describes her personality. For example, in the excerpt from the short story "How Far She Went," notice the way an Impala—a large, rugged practical car—is really an extension of a particular woman who, in a rage, is "driven" to her actions. In Trey Hunigan's essay (page 175), a father is so closely associated with gadgets that a Dustbuster seems almost like another arm.

NUGGETS

FROM A STORY IN PROGRESS "HOWARD"

animal = giraffe
kitchen utensil = corkscrew
color = brushed gold

Howard could stick his neck out like no one else I knew. He sometimes took risks for the sake of taking risks. But often what looked to everyone else like a foolish risk would end up being a sound investment. Not glittery, but subtle, like brushed gold. Howard was like that, a class act, except for his reasoning, which was circuitous at best and downright screwy most of the time.

KEVIN HARRIS

■

FROM THE ESSAY "MY FATHER THE DUST BUSTER"

I used to think my father loved his gadgets more than he loved me. Or at least as much. He sold life insurance for a living, which seemed an abstract, sad profession to me, and when I got older, I began to realize that it was more that he appreciated the solidness and realness of things than that he actually loved them. And nothing was realer to my dad than a new gadget.

After all, like all humans, my mother and I were composed of mostly water, and no one knew more than he, an insurance salesman, how quickly a life could be flushed out of a person. But a gadget was something else altogether, infinitely fixable, ready to take on the lowliest household task with an electric buzz of glee.

I remember my father and his first Dustbuster waking me early one Saturday morning, as smiling and open mouthed, both of them inched their way around my headboard. . . .

TREY HUNIGAN

ARTIFACTS

ELLA, IN A SQUARE APRON, ALONG HIGHWAY 80

She's a copperheaded waitress,
tired and sharp-worded, she hides
her bad brown tooth behind a wicked
smile, and flicks her ass
out of habit, to fend off the pass
that passes for affection.
She keeps her mind the way men
keep a knife—keen to strip the game
down to her size. She has a thin spine,

swallows her eggs cold, and tells lies.
She slaps a wet rag at the truck drivers
if they should complain. She understands
the necessity for pain, turns away
the smaller tips, out of pride, and
keeps a flask under the counter. Once,
she shot a lover who misused her child.
Before she got out of jail, the courts had pounced
and given the child away. Like some isolated lake,
her flat blue eyes take care of their own stark
bottoms. Her hands are nervous, curled, ready
to scrape.
The common woman is as common as a rattlesnake.

JUDY GRAHN

FROM THE SHORT STORY "HOW FAR SHE WENT"

Furious, she ran to her car, past the barking dog, this time leaving him
behind, driving after them, horn blowing nonstop, to get back what was
not theirs. She drove after them knowing what they did not know, that
all roads beyond that point dead-ended. She surprised them, swinging
the Impala across their path, cutting them off; let them hit it!

MARY HOOD

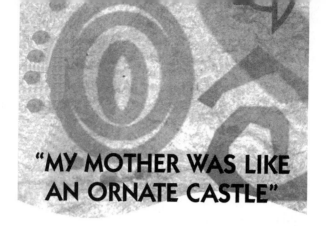

"MY MOTHER WAS LIKE AN ORNATE CASTLE"

ew topics engage the imagination of writers as much as relationships. Rarely simple, relationships with family, friends, and lovers bring out the best and worst in all of us. We run from relationships and work at relationships. Some of us take our relationships with us into therapy. Even for those who lead relatively isolated lives, past relationships can be a powerful, life-defining force—sometimes defining enough to send us into hiding.

We write books and essays about relationships and feature them in sitcoms and epic tragedies: Romeo and Juliet, Oedipus and Creon, Cain and Abel, Burt and Loni, Julia and Lyle. Comic, tragic, romantic, existential; light, heavy, murderous, meaningless. Relationships are what we are doing when we're not working or recovering from work.

The following exercises prompt you to explore relationships by comparing them to other things and processes and to muse on relationships that never happened.

PANNING INSTRUCTIONS

1. Fill in the following blanks with specific relationships—real or imagined— and with *unexpected* similes (using *like* or *as* to join two different things). For example: My relationship with *my mother* was like *an ornate castle*.

• My relationship with _____ is/was like _____

  _____

  _____.

• My relationship with _____ is/was like _____

  _____

  _____.

*   My relationship with _____ is/was like _____

_____

_____.

2.   Using one of the similes you have just created as a springboard or focus, **freewrite** or **free associate** reasons, justifications, or explanations for this comparison. For example: *My relationship with my mother was like an ornate castle because it was full of hidden passages and royalty.*

3.   Now begin a poem, story, or essay using the material you generated. Notice how Janeen Miller's excerpt (page 179) would probably lead to a poem because of the imagery she uses.

EXCAVATING INSTRUCTIONS

Some of our most romantic musings center on relationships that, for whatever reason, *didn't* materialize. Someone might find herself occasionally wondering how her life might have turned out differently if she had dated that person she could never even work up her nerve to speak to. Someone else might wonder what kind of relationship he would have had with his mother, who died when he was only two.

Begin an essay, story, or poem that explores either a real or fictional relationship that *never happened* but might have changed everything if it had.

NUGGETS

LOVER'S CANVAS

A painting layered over to cover mistakes
the rough brush strokes so much paint spent
wasted in the effort turpentine couldn't even
dissolve it all the way
we did this one thing together right
the laying it on
the thick way we tried to cover up the past and
paint it over ending up with
the canvas of our relationship
one ruined city after another

MARIAM ROMELLO

FROM THE PANNING INSTRUCTIONS

My relationship with my mother is like the weather on an early spring day. It begins with the promise of freshness, warmth, renewal. With confidence I put on the shorts and T-shirt that were long hidden in the bottom of a drawer and rush outside.

For the first time in months, the sun feels warm on my skin. The birds sing their excitement. The sky is azure blue. I begin to trust that spring is really here. . . .

Puffy white clouds slowly build in the west. First one or two, then just as quickly, a dozen. I ignore them. By noon they darken and cover the sky. A cool breeze rises. I tell myself it will pass quickly. I want to trust this day.

By mid-day I can no longer deny the change. . . .

JANEEN MILLER

 **ARTIFACTS**

FROM THE ESSAY "SOMEWHERE IN THE EIGHTIES"

One day, during a quiet moment in what was to prove our last visit together before her death, my grandmother looked up from her coffee and spoke of her son, breaking a virtual silence of decades in so simple a manner that I knew she'd been asking the question of herself for thirty-some years. "I suppose you've often wondered," she said, "what would have happened if your father had been the one to live, if he'd been the one to raise you. . . ."

The only formal photograph of my family that I have ever seen was taken on Easter, 1953. My father, hair already whitening, is holding me; my mother stands beside him; my two sisters stand in front, and my yet-unborn brother is indicated only the curve of my mother's coat. As I study this image, and think of the funeral that will take place five months later, I am still unable to wonder much about what might have been. . . .

COLETTE BROOKS

RETURNING FROM THE DEAD

As children we're afraid of the monsters that hide under our beds and in dark closets. A three-year-old will shoo a ghost out the back door with the same serious sense of purpose he applies to trying on his mother's high heels. As we get older, our fears often become more abstract. We say we're "afraid" of getting fired, of spending a weekend alone, of bouncing a check. But we are no less guided by our fears than we are as children.

Fear is one of our most potent emotional and imaginative processes and is as much a motivator as it is an obstacle to motivation. Identify a person's fears and you know perhaps the most important thing about him. As such, fear is a rich source for writing ideas.

PANNING INSTRUCTIONS

1. **List** things you fear or should fear or have feared. Try to be as playful and loose as you can be in listing things, occasionally adding something unlikely or ridiculous just for fun. Try to mix the extraordinary with the ordinary, the expected with the unexpected, for example:

Things I Fear

Bats
Snakes
The dead
The unknown
The undead
The unsaid
The insane
The shower

The half-baked
Omelette recipes
Polkas
Asphyxiation
Green pants
Right angles
Heights
Spiders
Wood paneling
Guys named Tad
Cellophane
The sadly religious
The happily married
Wax buildup

2.   Next, combine some of these fears in a story, poem, or essay. For example:

Green Pants

When I was ten
learning the polka was like being
strangled by a pair of green pants.
I feared asphyxiation even then.
I feared right angles and the sadly religious
guy named Tad who taught the polka
and was as insane as the undead.

EXCAVATING INSTRUCTIONS

The source of all fear is perhaps death itself, for death represents the ultimate unknown. Writers in a number of genres have tried creatively to transcend death or otherwise deal with it by inventing heavens and hells and afterlives, or by inventing ways to sidestep, avoid, or in some way to control death—for example, Faust or Superman. Most horror stories, from *Dracula* and *Franken-stein* to *The Return of The Living Dead,* are elaborate attempts to transcend death.

Begin a story, poem, or essay in which you return from the dead after several years. **Freewrite** about what you would want to do immediately after your resurrection, as Peggy Bair does in "Upon Awakening Halloween Night" (page 182). (Horror movies often depict the returning dead as being angry and vengeful. Would you be?)

NUGGETS

UPON AWAKENING HALLOWEEN NIGHT

Oh, paradise!
Disgusting perfection, hideous divinity,
generation upon eon of boring bliss.
I wrench myself awake, rub dirt from my eyes,
test antique knees.

My tongue aches for a glass of wine!
For dry summer meadows and bursting weeping berries.
And where are you, cat of Ramses? You who have died
nine thousand deaths, still bounding through nine thousand lives.

Where is the cat who remembers Egypt?
Only you can understand how it is to
love the world in that screw-you sort of way.

PEGGY BAIR

ARTIFACTS

FROM THE POEM "LADY LAZARUS"

"A miracle!"
That knocks me out.

There is a charge, a very large charge
For hearing of my heart—
It really goes.

And there is a charge, a very large charge
For a word or a touch
Or a bit of blood

Or a piece of my clothes or hair. . . .

SYLVIA PLATH

From the Novel *Ironweed*

None of the graves were yet marked with headstones, but a few were marked with an American flag on a small stick, or bunches of faded cloth flowers in clay pots. Rudy and Francis filled in one hollow, then another. Dead gladiolas, still vaguely yellow in their brown stage of death, drooped in a basket at the head of the grave of Louis (Daddy Big) Dugan, the Albany pool hustler who had died only a week or so ago from inhaling his own vomit. Daddy Big, trying futilely to memorize anew fading memories of how he used to apply topspin and reverse English to the cue ball, recognized Francis Phelan, even though he had not seen him in twenty years. . . .

Your son Billy saved my life, Daddy Big told Francis. Turned me upside down and kept me from chokin' to death in the street when I got sick. I died anyway, later. But it was nice of him, and I wish I could take back some of the lousy things I said to him. And let me personally give you a piece of advice. Never inhale your own vomit.

William Kennedy

AS RESTLESS AS PANTYHOSE

Whether we are describing feelings, places, or people, most of us have a natural tendency to compare. "I was as scared as I was when I got caught at the beach during that hurricane." "She pleaded like a hungry child." We compare to describe and make sense of the world. If one thing is "like" something else, then *nothing* can be too peculiar or unusual to comprehend.

While comparisons can help us understand and explain, they can also limit our vision. Overreliance upon likely comparisons—similes—can cause us to circumscribe, or draw a careful border, around our world. We all know a person who, upon tasting anything unusual for the first time, declares it "tastes just like chicken" or who seems incapable of traveling anywhere without comparing the new places to his hometown.

In these exercises, you'll experiment with making comparisons that will surprise you and increase your ability to make the kind of fresh connections that enrich writing.

PANNING INSTRUCTIONS

1.   The following is a list of adjectives set up to be turned into similes (comparisons using "like" or "as"). Complete each (in a couple of different ways, if you wish) quickly, without worrying too much whether your comparisons are original or not:

As orange as	Stumbling like a
As empty as	Running like a
As hungry as	Crying like a
As blue as	Laughing like a
As dull as	Smiling like a
As fragile as	Gathered together like a

As arrogant as	Singing like a
As rough as	Trembling like a
As regular as	Praying like a
As tentative as	Grinning like a
As pliant as	Sailing like a
As terrified as	Suffering like a
As eloquent as	Coughing like a
As reliable as	Stinking like a
As restless as	Mumbling like a
As confining as	Screaming like a
As pale as	Bowing like a
As sweet as	Flirting like a

2. Next, mix and match the adjectives and nouns, looking for interesting results as in the sample below:

Original Simile List

As restless as a salesman
As orange as Tang
As regular as taxes
As hungry as a gorilla
As pale as pantyhose
Smiling like a schoolgirl
Grinning like a lunatic

Mix and Match Simile List

As restless as pantyhose
As orange as taxes
As regular as a salesman
As hungry as Tang
As pale as a gorilla
Smiling like a lunatic
Grinning like a schoolgirl

3. Begin a story, poem, or essay with one or more of the unusual similes you have created.

EXCAVATING INSTRUCTIONS

1. Try mixing the adjectives and nouns you worked with above to create new metaphors as in the sample list below. (A metaphor is an assertion that one thing *is* another thing.)

Original List

As rough as sandpaper
As confining as an elevator
As tentative as a first kiss
As reliable as a new car
Stumbling like a drunk
Gathered together like a prayer group

Mix and Match Metaphor List

A first kiss is sandpaper.
My prayer group is an elevator.
The drunk is a new car.

2.   Begin an essay, poem, or story in which you work with one of the metaphors you have created, extending its definition and relevancy throughout the piece.

NUGGETS

A start on the poem "Family"

My sister is as fragile as a pill box
She makes herself tiny and empty
as yesterday's blue pliant moon

My brother is as restless
as an orange sock spinning
free from the dryer

I am praying like the taxman

Dave Thurman

From the essay "Dorm Room"

My dorm room is a bouquet. The florist has thrown it all in—the wild blues of laundry, the splashy orange of notebooks, the dry green of telephone lines. The fragrance lures them in from the hallway—the rich, delicate rendering of my roommate's boyfriend's cheap cologne, the slice of pepperoni pizza she saved from lunch, my Jergens skin cream. . . .

Rachel Kaplan

ARTIFACTS

Harlem

What happens to a dream deferred?

Does it dry up
like a raisin in the sun?
Or fester like a sore—

And then run?
Does it stink like rotten meat?
Or crust and sugar over—
like a syrupy sweet?

Maybe it just sags like a heavy load.
Or does it explode?

Langston Hughes

ARTFUL LYING

reative writers have a license to lie in the interest of truth, to prevaricate in the service of beauty. In the realms of poetry and fiction, it's okay to say that something happened when it didn't, to say that something is when it isn't—so long as the result moves the reader closer to what the writer really, and honestly, wants to express. However, the best writing is always in some sense emotionally honest. To say, "I was so lonely I picked up the telephone and called the whole state of Minnesota," is factually a lie, but perhaps emotionally close to the truth.

The following assignment asks you to commit two kinds of lies in the interest of art: public lies and private lies. Private lies are those focusing on you; public lies concern everything else. A typical private lie might be that you are younger or older than you are; a typical public lie might be that Richard Nixon had a twin sister.

PANNING INSTRUCTIONS

Freewrite for four to five minutes on things you wish you had done or could do. Mix the possible ("I wish I had visited the Grand Canyon") with the impossible ("I wish I could fly" or "I wish I had been Warren B. Harding"). Repeat the prompts "I wish I had" or "I wish I could" when you get stuck; for example:

> *I wish I had published a book by the time I was thirty, I wish I had learned to scuba dive, I wish I had stayed in California, I wish I could change color, I wish I could achieve a balance between art and life, I wish I had studied acting.*

Now begin a story, poem, or essay by claiming you did do all that you said you wish you had done or could do:

I published a book when I was thirty and lived in California. I learned how to scuba dive, I studied acting, and I finally figured out how to balance life and art and how to change color.

Develop your piece around the *impossible* accomplishments. For example, in the example above, the writer might take off on the idea of changing color as follows:

Changing color, it might surprise you to learn, wasn't the hardest accomplishment, though I needed to do everything else first. When I was scuba diving off Key Largo, I was so taken by the colorful fish, I had, I suppose, a kind of revelation, what some would call "rapture of the deep. . . ."

EXCAVATING INSTRUCTIONS

Try to write a poem, short piece of fiction, or creative nonfiction in which every line or sentence contains a personal lie or a lie about public facts. (If you write a poem, try alternating personal and public lies, as Tony Russo does in his poem "Third Grade," below.) Additionally, tell lies that don't necessarily benefit you.

NUGGETS

THIRD GRADE

I broke every window in my high school
because my English teacher got married.
They made Europe into a U.S. territory and I got tickets
for the state of Spain. The Spanish love marshmallows
and I bought the trees on which they grow.
My English teacher used to call me her wonder boy
and she told me the real conjugation of the word love
was love, have loved, and have not. One amendment to
the constitution says that we have the right
to lie if we don't like the truth. I don't.

TONY RUSSO

ARTIFACTS

FROM THE SHORT STORY "I'M TELLING YOU THE TRUTH"

Everyone who is interested in seeing the camel pass through the eye of the needle should inscribe his name on the list of patrons for the Niklaus Experiment.

Disassociated from a group of death-dealing scientists, the kind who manipulate uranium, cobalt, and hydrogen, Arpad Niklaus is guiding his present research toward a charitable and radically humanitarian end: the salvation of the souls of the rich.

He proposes a scientific plan to disintegrate a camel and make it pass in a stream of electrons through a needle's eye. . . .

JUAN JOSE ARREOLA
(TRANSLATED BY GEORGE B. SCHADE)

IMPLAUSIBLE CAUSES AND UNLIKELY EFFECTS

I n the natural course of things, any accident, event, development, phenomenon, or trend was caused by something else, just as any change from the status quo will produce one or several effects. Analysis of causes and effects is more often associated with science, engineering, and the insurance industry than with creative writing, but such analysis with a dash of imagination can produce some very engaging writing, including science fiction and mystery novels.

Anyone who has wondered how that single shoe found its way to the edge of the highway or how that car lost its sideview mirror has already begun the same process that mystery writers use to figure out how the murderer got in and out of the well-guarded hospital room. Anyone who has asked "What would it be like to be invisible for a day?" has already begun the process by which science fiction writers explore their many "what ifs." Poets and essayists also use such questions to begin poems and advance ideas. When William Stafford was asked how he came up with an idea for a poem wherein a bird spirals out of control, he said that one day he saw a bird and wondered how it would fly if it had only one wing. Of course it would fall, he realized, but for a while it would surely spiral.

The following exercises ask you to imaginatively indulge your natural curiosity and your prophetic powers to account for several extraordinary causes and effects.

OPANNING INSTRUCTIONS

Choose one or several of the following idea starters and imaginatively account for the causes of the phenomena described and/or provide a creative sequence of effects.

1. Two P.M. His wife never slept this late. (Why now?)

2.   Someone had set his stuffed owl on fire. (Who and why?)

3.   It would have been a perfect morning had she not noticed the neighbor's lawn chair sitting on her bed of ornamental cabbage. (How'd it get there? What happened?)

4.   The note simply said "There are more where these came from." The only other things in the envelope were three perfectly clipped fingernails. (Whose fingernails? What's the meaning?)

5.   This time she was grateful her husband hadn't noticed that she was wearing a new dress. (Why?)

6.   The boys seemed to be kicking a large Bible between the two of them. (Why?)

7.   The letter from the IRS said his returns for the last three years would be examined. (What was his reaction?)

8.   In the middle of the meeting, for no reason she could discern, she told her boss, "You have a lovely smile." (What happened?)

9.   The ad he put in the paper included his phone number and simply said, "Send in the clowns." (What happened?)

10. It was tough fitting all those helium balloons in the station wagon. (What happened?)

EXCAVATING INSTRUCTIONS

Sometimes extraordinary effects result from very ordinary occurrences, and very common results have very uncommon antecedents. Mispronouncing someone's name, or calling someone by the wrong name, can set off a lethal sequence of events. The simple salad your host presents to you might be the culmination of hellish dramas (for example, the first grocery store she went to might have been out of lettuce, the second store carried only lettuce that was so thoroughly wilted, it couldn't be revived, and not one store in the whole town had decent cucumbers).

   In this exercise, choose an ordinary cause, such as a change of address, or an ordinary effect, such as at last mastering the ability to whistle, as a subject and begin a story, poem, or essay that exposes or describes unlikely or dramatic antecedents or consequences. In Michael Jenkins's "One Way of Looking at It," notice how the ongoing effects of a dog bite changed the fortunes of a mail carrier (see page 193).

NUGGETS

FROM THE SHORT STORY IN PROGRESS "ONE WAY OF LOOKING AT IT"

I asked him what I thought to be a fairly typical question, one people must always ask of postmen: "Ever been bitten by a dog?"

He took a bite out of his grilled cheese sandwich and thought about my question as he chewed. "Oh, not too much trouble with dogs," he said. "Just once."

I had expected a couple of impassioned dog stories and was pleasantly surprised that Oscar had none.

But then he said, "Yep, a dog I'd know for maybe eight years. Surprised the bejesus out of me. Nice people, the owners."

"What happened?"

"Damnedest thing. I just put the mail in their box, same as I had done for years. Sometimes I'd see the dog, not a very big fella, a terrier of some sort, sometimes he wouldn't even come to the door. I'd petted that dog on hundreds of occasions. He knew me. Knew what I smelled like. But that day I put the mail in the box, as I said, and I hear the screen door close and next thing you know this little old dog bit me on the rear end."

Oscar laughed at this and shook his head.

He was silent after that, so I assumed he'd finished talking about it. I was preparing to change the subject and ask him about postal rates when he continued: "I really hated like the dickens to sue those folks. Nice people, as I said."

"You sued them?" It was hard to imagine this kindly man suing anybody, and from his description there didn't seem like much to sue over.

"Well, it wasn't so much me. The union, you know. Plus my co-workers, my boss. They thought I should. After I got out of the hospital . . ."

"Hospital?" I asked. "Why were you in the hospital?"

"Oh, one thing and another. Skin graft. Some muscle damage."

"From what?" I asked, thinking he was talking about something else now.

"Why the dog bite of course. That little fella hung on. Took a big bite out of my rear end. I was on my stomach for seven weeks. . . ."

"So you used the money from the lawsuit to buy the property in Santa Monica."

"That's right. And then I sold it and bought two more properties with the proceeds. My son manages one building. We made enough money to buy a place up in Malibu."

"Malibu? You bought a house in Malibu and three buildings in Santa Monica, all because of this dog bite?"

Oscar took a sip from his soda and looked at me with what seemed like genuine surprise.

"You know, I never thought of it that way. But you're right. That's certainly one way of looking at it."

MICHAEL JENKINS

 **ARTIFACTS**

FROM THE SHORT STORY "ANY MINUTE MOM SHOULD COME BLASTING THROUGH THE DOOR"

Mom died in the middle of making me a sandwich. If I had known it was going to kill her, I never would have asked. It never killed her before to make a sandwich, so why all of a sudden. My dad didn't understand it either. But we don't talk about it too much. Sometimes we try. Sometimes it's just the two of us at dinner, and things are almost good.

But only sometimes.

DAVID ORDAN

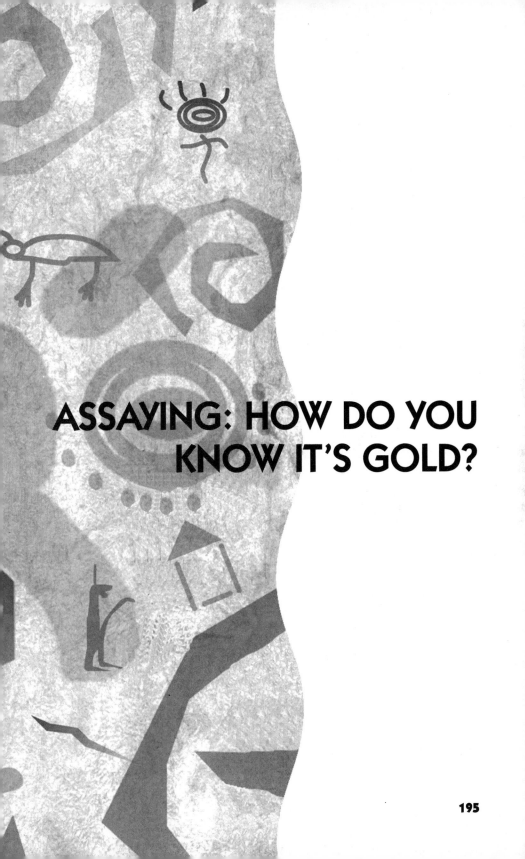

ASSAYING: HOW DO YOU KNOW IT'S GOLD?

There was one person in the camp, and only one, who had seen gold in pieces new from the earth. This was Jenny Wimmer. Not only had Jenny seen virgin gold, but she knew how women tested it in their backwoods kitchens. . . .

Jenny took Jim's bits of metal and soaked them in vinegar. They came out unhurt. Now, she told the men, she would try a test more severe. Jenny was boiling a kettle of soap, strong lye soap that would take the dirt and sweat out of men's work clothes. She dropped some bits of metal into her lye vat and let it boil all day and simmer all night. Nothing but gold, said Jenny, could stand the test.

FROM *GOLDEN DREAMS,* BY GWEN BRISTOW

If you have attempted several of the exercises in this book, you have generated many ideas and beginnings for stories, poems, and essays. *Beginnings, in the way we are using the term here, are not necessarily the same as the starts of poems, stories, or essays. Your beginnings may in fact end up in the middle or end of your final poem, story, or essay, or they might be replaced altogether with new writing.* Perhaps you have even gone beyond beginnings to fully develop several pieces. But if you haven't, a question you're likely to have at this point is, "What do I do with all this writing?"

What you do with the material you've generated is, of course, up to you. You may have had fun doing the exercises for their own sake, and that's enough for now. On the other hand, you may want to continue to work on a piece and shape it into a specific form—a story, poem, or essay. Review "From Nuggets to Artifacts: What Form Should You Choose?" on page 20. But first you need to decide which pieces to work on further. How can you tell which exercises resulted in the most promising material?

Unlike the methods for assaying metals for gold, there is no guaranteed way of determining beforehand whether a piece of writing contains gold. In the realm of art and creativity, it's nearly impossible to get any two people to agree on criteria for evaluating whether something is good. Even if they reach an agreement, the next hurdle is getting these same people to agree that something does or doesn't *meet* the criteria. Add to these difficulties the fact that the exercises being looked at here are simply beginnings, and it's clear that any "objective" criteria that might be applied to a finished piece of writing should be considered only very cautiously.

Still, you need some way to begin to sift through the sand and rock and jackrabbit bones you have dug up. The following recommendations, then, are given in the spirit of helping you to separate the gold from the dross.

Respect how you feel about a beginning. If you are in love with something you wrote and you have a tremendous hunch that it could pan out, you almost have no choice but to pursue it. Your task and problem here are similar to Michelangelo's when he tried to find the slabs of Carrara marble that would contain his visions for his sculptures. Sometimes he would have a two-ton piece of marble carted back to his studio and work on the piece for days, only to discover that his figures would not emerge from the marble the way he had imagined them. He had no choice but to destroy these and return to the quarry. Fortunately, more often than not, Michelangelo's instincts were correct, and undoubtedly he got better at choosing with time and experience. Since your medium is words, the stakes are not quite as high in choosing the rough beginnings that will flourish into finished stories, poems, or essays.

Show your work to someone you respect. Obviously, if you are taking a writing class, the writing instructor would probably fill this role as might classmates whose opinions you trust. Most experienced writers and writing teachers will be able to look over your exercises and pick out a few that seem promising, in addition to offering some tips for how to develop the pieces. Otherwise, consider showing your work to someone whose opinion you value and who, ideally, reads extensively or is very interested in writing. People who are not devoted friends will probably be reluctant to comment on your work in general but may feel better about looking over a few beginnings and choosing the ones that they'd like to see developed. Be careful about showing personal pieces to the people that they are about, especially too early in the process. Their opinions about the work may be distorted by any personal biases they have.

Does It Glitter: Freshness and Originality

Aside from your own or someone else's sense about your beginnings, the following factors might suggest that you continue.

The Topic or Piece of Writing Keeps Coming Back to You

If something you've written virtually haunts you, this may be a strong indication that you should develop it. In the course of freewriting once, one of the coauthors wrote the phrase "It was no ordinary parasol, officer." The sound and rhythm of that odd phrase returned to him almost every time he sat down to write. It would even come to him as he sat watching a movie. The problem was that it made no sense to him. It was just an intriguing fragment. But he had this powerful sense that it could become something. He worked on it off and on for nearly two years and finally finished and ultimately published a poem about a prostitute in the French Quarter of New Orleans. He did not work nonstop on this piece for two years. He worked on other pieces as well, and so should you even if one beginning particularly haunts you.

You Find Yourself "Working" on the Piece Without Deliberately Trying To

Perhaps you began the "At the Checkout Line" exercise and were delighted with some of the items you placed upon the imaginary conveyor belt—to such a degree that while at work on your job you imagined yet other odd and fascinating items on it . . . a buffalo's beard, a pirate's eyepatch, an inflatable Pat Sajak. Or perhaps you began describing your best friend's talent at mixing up people's names while doing "The Evolution of Mini-Skills" exercise, and now you are on the phone talking to someone else about this realization, supplying examples, elaborating. In both instances, it might be better to stop what you're doing, if you can, and develop the piece. In such cases, your writing imagination is still crackling synapses, and it's always a shame to waste that kind of energy.

The Beginning of the Piece Helped You Discover Something You Didn't Know about Yourself or Someone Else or the Human Condition

Many of the preceding writing exercises ask you to reflect about yourself, your sense of the world, as well as your experiences in it. In completing the "Mixing Relationships" exercise, perhaps you discovered that there are a number of things that you don't do with your spouse that you do with others—perhaps for no good reason. The exercise allowed you to touch on this, but developing the piece might show you the way to work through it, at least on paper. Such realizations in writing make for very powerful stories, poems, and essays. (Writing can be and is therapeutic for many, though we don't recommend restricting it to that role.)

You Are Intrigued by an Odd or Original Connection You Have Made between Two Seemingly Very Different Things

The essence of metaphor is transformation, relating one aspect of experience to another and thereby altering both; for example, Emily Dickinson imagined the hummingbird as a mail carrier from Tunisia; Ezra Pound imagined the faces of people at a subway station as "white petals on a wet black bough." In both cases, two very different realities are related, and the result enriches our perception and sense of both. Many of the preceding exercises involve you in metaphors of one kind or another, and it is very likely that you came up with metaphors that for the first time connected two very different phenomena in a rewarding fashion. One student, for example, while doing the "Air Travel: Unlikely Seatmates" exercise, wrote: "In each seat, something is boiling or baking or frying. . . ." This is a very original way of looking at one's fellow passengers on an airplane, and it's easy to see how he could further develop this idea by citing specific passengers and talking about how they are "cooking" their emotions about the flight.

You Introduced a Character You Like a Great Deal and Are Concerned about What Might Happen to Her or Him

In the course of completing exercises involving descriptions of people, real and fictional, you may on occasion find yourself invested in a character's fate. You wonder how the character you've created will handle a certain problem. As you struggle through your own daily dilemmas, you find yourself anticipating the way one of your characters might react. Fiction writers often care nearly as much about the characters they've created as they do about their real friends and family. (In the course of writing the novel *Beloved,* Toni Morrison has said she felt that her characters literally had moved in with her.) This is only natural since in a very real sense the writer gives birth to characters and cares as only a parent can care.

If you have such feelings about a character or characters you've brought to life on paper, this is a good sign that you should stick with the piece.

You Introduced a Character You Dislike and Are Concerned about the Damage He or She May Do

Sometimes we create people whom we hope *never* to meet in real life. In the process of completing "The Spice Rack" exercise, one student wrote "Senor Cumin was as subtly evil as he was strong, and his lies were as toxic as his breath. He told Saffron Salido that her grandfather had cursed her on his death bed, knowing that such a curse lasts longer than simple profanity." While total villains are often one dimensional and can easily fall into the category of clichéd or stock characters; brooding, neurotic, mean-spirited, narcissistic, vindictive people often set stories into motion and, if fully developed, can make wonderful characters.

As a writer, it's your job to see the humanity in even the most loathsome of creations. While you may not love these creatures, to avoid creating clichéd characters, it's important that you *understand* them and their motivations and realize that we *all* have something in common. Even a mass murderer probably has a favorite breakfast cereal, not to mention a mother, father, or sibling who worries about him.

If you have created a character that you don't particularly like but who nevertheless intrigues you, you may very well have the beginnings of a compelling piece of writing.

You Love the Sound of the Words You've Strung Together

Beginning writing efforts are often marked by flourishes of remarkable words, phrases, and rhythms. Sometimes the meanings are not all that satisfying, but the sounds may be beautiful and compelling, and this may signal that you should continue on with the piece. For example, while **listing** uncelebrated important occasions for the Panning exercise of "Party Invitations," one student wrote:

1. My eighteenth birthday.
2. The time I got down from the tree by myself.
3. The time I got up from my moods by myself.
4. The time I got my moods out of the trees, out of the woods, out of myself.

Notice how sound, particularly repetition, begins to take over the list, resulting in a resonant and lovely line in the end.

You Feel Like You Could Write a Lot More about This

While your final essays, stories, and poems will vary in length greatly—many writers feel that each piece they write has its own natural length—if you feel you *could* write a lot initially on the subject, that is certainly a good sign. This means that the topic has sparked something that resonates with either your imagination, your life experience, or a combination of the two.

You may end up using a small fraction of all of this outpouring of words, but for most writers it is generally easier to edit by cutting back than by adding on to a meager start.

You're Dying to Send/Show the Piece to Others

Wanting to share work is a clear sign that a writer is excited about her material. At heart, most adults are not so different from children who eagerly choose what amazing new thing to bring in to show off to their classmates for show-and-tell. If you want to share your work, usually this means there is something in it worth working on further.

Of course, there are exceptions. Perhaps you want to show someone your initial work on "Mixing Relationships" strictly because you think he'll get a kick out of the fact that he appears in it. Still, even in these kinds of cases, that genuine spark of interest may be there.

You Feel That What You've Written Is Fresh or Original

With respect to writing, most people agree that freshness, originality, and an element of surprise are factors in what they characterize as "creative." Ben Jonson, a seventeenth-century English writer and scholar, characterized poetry as "What has been oft thought but ne'r so well expressed." In so saying, Jonson relieves poets of the obligation of coming up with new ideas and focuses on the perhaps infinite number of ways that ideas can be expressed.

To illustrate this idea, consider that most of us were required to write a "What I Did This Summer" essay at some point in our school careers. While the subject matter for these essays is largely the same among classmates—camp, swimming pools, summer jobs—the ways in which we wrote our stories, those details we chose to highlight and those we chose to omit, are what gave each piece its own flavor and perhaps its shot at originality. Compare, for example, the first paragraph of the following hypothetical "What I Did This Summer" essays written by two sixth-graders who had largely the same summer experiences:

1. *I went to camp this summer, which was interesting. I had never been to camp before and I enjoyed meeting new people. I slept in a bunk house with five other girls. I went sailing and learned how to macrame, which really is more boring than it might sound. I made a new friend who was very nice. We did a lot of activities together, which made everything a little more interesting than it was before. It's important to have a good friend at camp.*

2. *Has anyone ever tried to convince you that tying knots is fun? How about sitting on a stagnant pond waiting for a gust of wind that never comes? Well I spent the summer waiting to be convinced that either of these activities were fun. At least I made a friend, Bobbie. Finally, we got smart*

and started hiding behind the bunk and reading her sister's old issues of Seventeen *when it was time for knot-tying class—whoops, I mean macrame.*

Most people would say that the second sixth-grader's beginning is much more compelling that the first's. The difference in the two lies in the freshness of detail. Notice how the first writer relies heavily on words like "boring," "interesting," and even "nice" that are overused and not as specific as they could be. She seems to be merely fulfilling the assignment instead of having fun with it.

The second writer, on the other hand, seems more engaged with her material. While she apparently found macrame at least as boring as the first writer did, she doesn't bore the reader with her description of it. Instead she pokes fun, calling it "knot tying" and finally lets us in on the joke. While the first writer *tells* us that her friendship was important to her, the second writer *shows* us what the friendship was like and how it helped redeem camp for her. Finally, notice that she *leaves out* details that are not particularly telling, for example that she slept in a bunk house and met a lot of new people. As she focused on the liveliest part of her camp experience, the more typical details naturally vanished.

In your own writing, look for pieces that have this kind of freshness or seem capable of it. The situation itself need not be unusual as long as your rendering of it causes the reader to look at it in a new way.

You Believe That What You've Written Honestly Expresses Some of Your Feelings

Whether you're working on fiction, poetry, or creative nonfiction, honesty of expression is something that is equally important. By *honesty,* we don't mean that you only write about what *really* happened. Actual events and experiences don't always translate into the best poem or story. Even essays usually benefit from selective editing of the facts.

Writing that is emotionally honest doesn't gloss over feelings, even those that may disturb the writer. Writing that is emotionally honest isn't always neat or pretty, but it is always emotionally *true.*

In looking over her work on "The Briefcase," one writer, who was adopted as an infant, came across the following passage that she had written about a photograph of herself and her birth mother and that she had carried in her purse since their "reunion" a year before:

Our faces squeeze close as we grin into the camera, faking delight at the similarity of our features. That crooked grin I always wondered about. Our reunion. We pretend this is it—family. I never thought I'd meet you, first, fleeting mother. We are an odd match, more like two strangers who resemble each other than relatives. You are not the one I call mother. I don't know if I want to see you again. I don't know why I save this photograph.

Although this passage made her uncomfortable, she felt that it expressed her conflicted feelings in an emotionally honest way and that the piece might be rich material for developing into an essay or poem.

Honesty of expression also does not include sentimentality, which is the emotional equivalent of a cliché (see the section on "Clichéd Emotions: Sentimentality" on page 205) and used more often to manipulate and hide emotions than to express them.

What You've Written Has Energy

Some writing moves; some writing sits. Energetic writing engages language. If your passages contain strong **active verbs** (*yell, whisper, leap, crawl, swarm*), have sentences that vary in length and form, and show a sense of wordplay throughout, these passages ask to live, and you should keep them alive by further developing them.

One writer came across this passage when reading over her initial work on "First Times":

My first guitar lesson was my last guitar lesson. I dragged that case around with me on and off three buses until I finally landed at his doorstep. My teacher. My nemesis. We sat in his living room while his three year old ran in and out reciting "Hickory Dickory Dock." He spent the first ten minutes lecturing me about being late, the next ten minutes tisk-tisking over the poor quality of my guitar strings, the next ten minutes squinting painfully at me while I strummed the chords he asked me to demonstrate.

While she wasn't quite sure where she was going yet, this passage felt alive to her and full of definite possibility. Not only was it rich in active verbs (*dragged, landed, ran, strummed*), the sentences varied in length and emphasis, and the repetitions ("My teacher. My nemesis.") added a sense of fun.

You've Created Tension or Conflict

You may think that the only kind of writing that requires conflict is fiction. But that's not really the case. Most writing that engages the reader contains tension or conflict of *some kind*; otherwise it can seem boring and facile. "That's nice," followed by a big yawn is not the reaction you want your readers to have.

The tension you create in your work may be purely internal, the narrator or a character explores a psychological or emotional concern. Or, it may be external, the narrator or a character is in conflict with another person or her environment. Often it is a combination of the two as Robert Mettler discovered as he reread the draft of his poem "Don't Ask Me," which was based on the "Quilting" exercise.

DON'T ASK ME

Don't ask me about the red.
The hem of the bright red orlon sweater
given me one Christmas
became hopelessly caught in a carnivorous
zipper and appalled my lovely third grade teacher.

Don't ask me about the white.
The collar of my best white shirt
should have had lipstick on it
but remained as virginal as a priest
who was really a saint.

ROBERT METTLER

In the first stanza, Robert describes literal tension of the sweater caught in the pant's zipper coupled with his teacher's reaction as well as his feelings for his "lovely" teacher, a whole brew of conflicts there. In the second stanza, the tensions arise in a different way. They are more abstract this time but still integral to the piece—the lack of the lipstick, the stain that *wasn't* there but should have been there. Tension existed in that discrepancy.

Consider working on pieces that are already on their way to creating one or another kind of tension or conflict. Such writing is ready for development.

HOW TO SORT REAL GOLD FROM FOOL'S GOLD

Be Sure That What You Have Written Doesn't Descend into Cliché

Clichéd Subjects.   While the subject you choose to write about doesn't have to be unusual, you should be aware that stock situations often give rise to clichés as much as you may try to avoid them. A clichéd subject is one that is so typical that it has become trite or a subject that is little more than a stereotype. For example, a story about a rich heiress named Tiffany who lives in Beverly Hills and has a Hispanic servant who is sleeping with the gardener is probably too clichéd for most writers to redeem. Similarly, an essay about the faithful collie you had as a boy, who constantly rescued you from danger, or a poem about the beauty of a rose stand little chance of exploring fresh territory.

Clichéd Characters.   Just as subjects can be clichéd, so can characterizations. A fat man who breathes heavily or sweats copiously; a chain-smoking (or sucker-sucking) private detective; a bored, station-wagon-driving housewife; and a recent immigrant who minces the language are all examples of stock or clichéd characters. It's not that such people do not exist; of course they do. It's just that they have been described so often and so *superficially* that they appear more as *stereotypes* than as real people. If you have begun to develop characters in your exercises, ferret out those that might be based on clichés by trying to imagine going out to lunch with each of them. Do they sit there like stick figures, only saying stock phrases? Do you find it hard to get them talking at all. It's the multidimensional or *rounded* characters with whom you'll be able to carry on the conversation, while the clichéd characters sit there silently chain-smoking or sweating, with no thoughts or feelings of their own to share.

Clichéd Emotions: Sentimentality.   While it has been said that writing of any worth *approaches* sentimentality, good writing steers just clear of plummeting into it in a blubbering mass.

Sentimentality is clichéd emotion. Nearly everybody wept when Ali McGraw died in *Love Story* and when Debra Winger slowly wasted away in *Terms of Endearment.* In the first case, a beautiful young woman was "shot down in her prime"; in the second case, we watched a young, vibrant mother of two adorable children die an agonizingly slow death. How could we not cry? Still, hours later, along with the enduring flavor of greasy popcorn, the taste of something else may have lingered, the residue of manipulation.

Good readers want to be genuinely moved, not manipulated. The difference is sometimes subtle. If your intention in writing a particular piece is strictly to move someone no matter which way your material seems to be naturally headed, you may be indulging in sentimentality.

Clichéd Language.   Perhaps the kind of cliché you are most familiar with is clichéd language. (If you worked on the exercise "The Cliché's the Thing," you experimented with identifying and exploiting clichéd language.) It is a cliché to write that someone "laughed until he cried" or had "ants in her pants." Sometimes we come up with what seem like wonderful expressions only to find out they are clichés.

The problem with clichés is that while they're often poetic-sounding, they're rarely completely accurate. Someone who writes that she had "stars in her eyes" the night she met her boyfriend may really have had beer in her stomach and a furious urge to dance with the next person who asked her. Someone who writes that he had "butterflies" when at the age of fifty-five he gave his first clarinet recital may have really been crunching so methodically on hard candy before he got on stage that all he could really think about was brushing his teeth.

Look through your own beginnings for situations, characters, and passages where you *might* have easily succumbed to cliché but didn't. The fact that you didn't shows you have a level of care and concern for this material that could help lead you to a strong finished piece.

Beware of What *Too Easily* Amuses or Impresses You

While many writers are their own toughest critics, these same writers can, on occasion, be too easily wooed by their own work. You may write a line that bowls you over with its humor or sentiment each time you read it only to find that it is nearly impossible to develop the piece in such a way that lets anyone else in on what is essentially a *private* joke or revelation.

Reading over the work he did on the exercise "Around the Water Cooler," one writer was delighted to discover he had created the following rumor about his office mate:

> *When working on the Davis account, Jeannine heard the word of God guiding her through the paperwork.*

Each time he read this passage over, he actually laughed aloud, thinking about the organized Jeannine with her briefcase and datebook being guided spiritually at work. Assuming that no one else could resist this image, the writer read the line to his wife, only to find her staring blankly back at him. He tried again, reading the line to another office mate; this time he received a polite half-smile and a mumbled question about whether he was ordering in for lunch. Why didn't anyone else get it?

The problem here is not that the image of a very practical person suddenly becoming spiritual *couldn't* be developed into a compelling description for a story, poem, or essay; it just hasn't been yet. The connections the writer has made in his mind haven't been made on the page because he is so taken with his insight, he hasn't seen that it is still strictly personal, *his* insight alone.

When you come across a private "joke" of some kind in your work, decide if the piece of writing is really meant to be private, an "in-joke" just you and perhaps one close friend gets, or if you're ready to step back and make the necessary connections to reveal its significance and meaning to the rest of the world.

SOME FINAL THOUGHTS

Now that you have been warned about what to avoid, remember that all writers, even the most well-published and experienced, at time descend into cliché or find themselves perhaps too easily impressed by their initial drafts. While it's part of every writer's job to learn to separate the gold from the dross, its unrealistic to expect every effort you make to pan out.

In fact, most practicing writers have drawers or file cabinets full of sand, rocks, and jackrabbit bones: short stories that never quite came to life; poems waiting for their finishing stanzas; essay ideas that didn't gel; even entire novels that for whatever reason didn't "work." Still, these efforts are much more than simple wastes of time. Even the stories, poems, and essays we will never finish can lead us mysteriously to our next stories, poems, or essays.

The important thing to remember is that as long as you are writing and engaging what is truly unique in you, you will always be approaching the best in all writing. Contrary to what many people think, the writing that is most affecting does not necessarily consist of the wildest and most extravagant imaginings by those who lead wild and extravagant lives, but instead consists of unique and very personal takes on everyday experiences.

F OR FURTHER READING

Over the last twenty years, many books have been published that provide instruction in the various forms of creative writing, including fiction, poetry, and creative nonfiction. Some of these books include instruction in all forms of creative writing, while others focus on one kind or another. There are also many books on creative writing that seek mainly to inspire and motivate writers and would-be writers. Such books combine philosophy, wisdom, experience, mysticism, and psychology.

The following list of books includes only those that offer some instruction in the techniques or theories of creative writing. While several also include what might be considered inspirational material, their main emphasis is on technique. This is by no means an exhaustive list. Check your library or bookstore for more titles.

Fiction

Barney, Anne and Pamela Painter. *What If: Writing Exercises for Fiction Writers*. New York: Harper Perennial, 1990.

Burnett, Hallie and Whit. *Fiction Writer's Handbook*. New York: HarperCollins, 1993.

Burroway, Janet. *Writing Fiction*. 3rd ed. New York: HarperCollins, 1992.

Cohen, Richard. *Writer's Mind: Crafting Fiction*. Lincolnwood (IL): NTC Publishing Group, 1995.

Gardner, John. *The Art of Fiction*. New York: Alfred A. Knopf, 1991.

Willis, Meredith Sue. *Personal Fiction Writing*. New York: Teachers & Writers Collaborative, 1993.

The Writer's Digest Handbook of Short Story Writing Volume II, Edited by Jean Fredette. Ohio: Writer's Digest Books, 1988.

Poetry

Drury, John. *Creating Poetry*. Ohio: Writer's Digest Books, 1991.

Rosenthal, M.L. *The Poet's Art*. New York: Norton, 1987.

The Teachers and Writers Handbook of Poetic Forms. Ed. Ron Padgett. New York: Teachers & Writers Collaborative, 1994.

Tucker, Shelly. *Writing Poetry*. New York: Scott Foresman, 1992.

Essays

Zinsser, William. *On Writing Well*. New York: HarperCollins, 1994.

Zinsser, William. *Writing to Learn*. New York: HarperCollins, 1993.

More Than One Format

Bishop, Wendy. *Working Words*. Mountain View (CA): Mayfield Publishing Company, 1992.

Burke, Carol and Molly Best Tinsley. *The Creative Process*. New York: St. Martins, 1993.

DeMaria, Robert. *The College Handbook of Creative Writing*. San Diego: Harcourt Brace Jovanovich, 1991.

Kubis, Pat and Bob Howland. *The Complete Guide to Writing Fiction and Non-fiction and Getting It Published*. Englewood Cliffs (NJ): Prentice Hall, 1990.

Mueller, Lavonne and Jerry D. Reynolds. *Creative Writing: Forms and Techniques*. Lincolnwood (IL): NTC Publishing Group, 1992.

Organizations

The following organizations offer many good resources for creative writers, including newsletters, magazines, and books that provide information on conferences, contests, and getting published, as well as other resources for creative writing teachers and students. Again, this list is by no means exhaustive:

Associated Writing Programs, George Mason University, Tallwood House, Mail Stop 1E3, Fairfax, VA 22030
Phone: (703) 993-4301

Poets and Writers, Inc., 72 Spring St., New York, NY 10012
Phone: (212) 226-3586

Teachers and Writers Collaborative, 5 Union Square West, New York, NY 10003
Phone: (212) 691-6590

ACKNOWLEDGMENTS

29 "Why I Will Not Get Out of Bed," by James Tate. © 1978 by James Tate. From "The Lost Pilot" published by The Ecco Press. Reprinted by Permission.

32 "Yard Sale" by Michael C. Smith appeared originally in *The Jacaranda Review,* vol. 3, no. 1 (1988). © 1988 by Michael C. Smith.

36 "The Coming Out of Ourselves Party" by James Tate appeared originally in *The Oblivion Ha-Ha.* © 1967, 1968, 1969, 1970. Published by The Atlantic Monthly Press. Reprinted by permission of the author.

40 Part Seven from "The White Album" from *The White Album* by Joan Didion. Copyright © 1979 by Joan Didion. Reprinted by permission of Farrar, Straus & Giroux, Inc.

42 "The Things They Carried" by Tim O'Brien appeared originally in *Esquire,* August 1986. Copyright © 1986 by Tim O'Brien. Reprinted by permission of the author.

46 "A Family Supper" by Kazuo Ishiguro appeared originally in *Esquire.* Reprinted by permission of Rogers, Coleridge & White Ltd.

49 Reprinted by permission of The Putnam Group from *Lighten Up, George* by Art Buchwald. Copyright © 1991 by Art Buchwald.

52 "My Papa's Waltz," copyright 1942 by Hearst Magazines, Inc. From *The Collected Poems of Theodore Roethke* by Theodore Roethke. Used by permission of Doubleday, a division of Bantam Doubleday Dell Publishing Group, Inc.

56 "Rosemary," copyright 1954 by Marianne Moore. Used by permission of Viking Penguin, a division of Penguin Books USA Inc.

57 The Natasha Sajé excerpt is taken from the poem "Creation Story" and is reprinted from *Red Under the Skin* by Natasha Sajé, by permission of the University of Pittsburgh Press, © 1994 by Natasha Sajé.

60   "The Elements" by Michael C. Smith appeared originally in *The Washington Review,* vol. 14, no. 3 (1988). © 1988 by Michael C. Smith.

64   "One Art" from *The Complete Poems 1927–1979* by Elizabeth Bishop. Copyright © 1979, 1983, by Alice Helen Methfessel. Reprinted by permission of Farrar, Straus & Giroux Inc.

68   William Carlos Williams: *Collected Poems 1909–1939 Vol. I.* Copyright 1938 by New Directions Publishing Corp. Reprinted by permission of New Directions Publishing Corp.

68   "Nothing to Do with Love," by Joyce Reiser Kornblatt, from *Nothing to Do with Love.* Reprinted by permission of the author.

71   An excerpt from the poem "Ode to My Socks" by Pablo Neruda from *Neruda and Valejo: Selected Poems,* edited and translated by Robert Bly. Published by Beacon Press. Copyright © 1967, 1976 by Robert Bly, reprinted with his permission.

72   "How It Is," copyright © 1975 by Maxine Kumin, from *Our Ground Time Here Will Be Brief* by Maxine Kumin. Used by permission of Viking Penguin, a division of Penguin Books USA Inc.

80   "Brothers and Sisters," by Stanley Plumly, from *Out-of-the-Body Travel.* Reprinted by permission of the author.

90   Excerpt from "A Good Man Is Hard to Find" in *A Good Man Is Hard to Find and Other Stories,* copyright 1953 by Flannery O'Connor and renewed 1981 by Regina O'Connor, reprinted by permission of Harcourt Brace & Company.

91   "This Is the Way" by Michael C. Smith appeared originally in *The Jacaranda Review,* vol. 10, no. 1 (1994). © 1994 by Michael C. Smith.

94   "Distance from Loved Ones" by James Tate appeared originally in *The Denver Quarterly.* Reprinted by permission.

96   From "Reading the Paper," by Ron Carlson, from *Sudden Fiction.* Reprinted by permission of the author.

101   Excerpt from "Neighbors," by Raymond Carver, from *Where I'm Calling From.* Published by The Atlantic Monthly Press. Reprinted by permission of the publisher.

101   "The Neighbor" by Russell Banks appeared originally in *Esquire.* Reprinted by permission.

104   Copyright © 1988 by The New York Times Company. Reprinted by permission.

110   Reprinted from *The Bridge of Sighs* by Steve Orlen by permission of Miami University Press. © 1992 by Miami University Press.

114   From "The Longest Day of the Year," by Ann Beattie, from *What Was Mine.* Published by Random House. © 1991 by Irony and Pity, Inc.

124 Excerpt from "Glossolalia," by David Jauss. The story appeared originally in *Shenandoah*. Reprinted by permission of the author.

127 Excerpt from "A & P," by John Updike, from *Pigeon Feathers and Other Stories* by John Updike. Published by Random House. Copyright © 1962 by John Updike.

131 Excerpt from "The Ocean" from *Shiloh and Other Stories* by Bobbie Ann Mason. Copyright © 1982 by Bobbie Ann Mason. Reprinted by permission of HarperCollinsPublishers, Inc.

137 From "Jamie," by Kathleen Maher. Appeared originally in *Fiction/86* (*Gargoyle Magazine*/Paycock Press). Reprinted by permission of the author.

142 "How to Cure Your Fever," by Thomas Lux. Appeared originally in *Emerson Review*. Reprinted by permission of the author.

147 Reprinted from *The Collected Poems of Weldon Kees,* edited by Donald Justice, by permission of the University of Nebraska Press. Copyright 1975, by the University of Nebraska Press.

150 "Elegy for Jane," copyright 1950 by Theodore Roethke. From *The Collected Poems of Theodore Roethke* by Theodore Roethke. Used by permission of Doubleday, a division of Bantam Doubleday Dell Publishing Group, Inc.

153 Reprinted from *The Collected Poems of Weldon Kees,* edited by Donald Justice, by permission of the University of Nebraska Press. Copyright 1975, by the University of Nebraska Press.

156 "Juggling" by Suzanne Greenberg appeared originally in *The Washington Review,* vol. 13, no. 5 (1988). © 1988 by Suzanne Greenberg.

159 "A Good Bet" by Suzanne Greenberg appeared originally in *Mississippi Review,* vol. 19, nos. 1 and 2 (1990). © 1990 by Suzanne Greenberg.

163 "The Geranium," copyright © 1963 by Beatrice Roethke, Administratrix of the Estate of Theodore Roethke. From *The Collected Poems of Theodore Roethke* by Theodore Roethke. Used by permission of Doubleday, a division of Bantam Doubleday Dell Publishing Group, Inc.

167 "old age sticks" is reprinted from *Complete Poems, 1904–1962,* by E. E. Cummings. Edited by George J. Firmage, by permission of Liveright Publishing Corporation. Copyright © 1958, 1986, 1991 by the Trustees for the E. E. Cummings Trust.

172 "My Brother, My Self" by Dick Schaap appeared originally in *Ms.* magazine in September 1986. Reprinted by permission of the author.

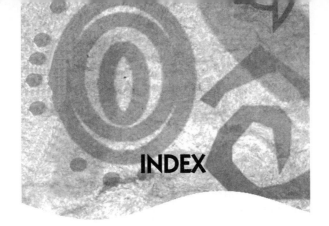

INDEX

A

Active verbs, 203
Adjectives, 161, 162
  turning, into similes, 184–87
Adverbs, 161
Albee, Edward, 20
Angelou, Maya, 20
Arreola, Juan Jose, 190

B

Bair, Peggy, 146, 181, 182
Banks, Russell, 101
Beattie, Ann, 113–14
Bishop, Elizabeth, 65
Blank lines, filling in, 73–74, 92–93, 140, 168–69
Bogazzi, Joanne, 75
Brainstorming, 10–11, 20, 26, 30–31, 58
Bristow, Gwen, 196
Britz, Mike, 110
Brooks, Colette, 179
Buchwald, Art, 49

C

Cabel, Irene, 158–59
Cain, Justin, 127
Callahan, Madelyn, 45
Carlson, Ron, 96–97
Carter, Sean, 63–64, 137, 142, 166

Carver, Raymond, 99, 101
Cause and effect, 92–94, 191–94
Celebrations, exploring, 34–37
Characters
  association in describing, 173–76
  clichéd, 205
  describing, 54–55, 132–34, 151, 168–72, 199–200
  writing description of, 54–55
Chekhov, Anton, 20
Choices, exploring reasons for, 26–29, 115–16
Chopin, Kate, 106, 107
Clichés, 144–46, 203, 204–6
Clustering, 12, 102, 108–9
Computer dictionary, 17
Computer thesaurus, 16–17
Conflict, creation of, 203–4
Crosswords, puzzling, 14–15
Cummings, E. E., 167
Cunningham, Michael, 150

D

Descriptive writing
  adding details in, 135–37, 151–53
  characters in, 54–55, 132–34, 168–76
Details
  adding, 135–37, 151–53
  developing, 88–91

Dialogue, 157–58
Diaries, 8
Dictionary, computer, 17
Didion, Joan, 20, 40–41
DoNofrio, Beverly, 76–77
Donohue, Angelin, 22, 56, 119, 120
Doubletalk, 157–59

E

Emotions
  clichéd, 205
  exploring, 26, 30–33, 63, 65, 202–3
Enagonio, Liz, 28, 99–100
Essays, writing, 22–23
Evaluation of writing, 197–204

F

Figurative language
  metaphors, 39, 89, 135–37, 161,
    185–86
  similes, 161, 177–79, 184–87
Filling in the blanks, 73–74, 92–93, 140,
  168–69
Focused freewriting, 9–10, 20
Folk remedies, 140–43
Francis, Jonathan, 147, 152–53
Free association, 12–14, 74, 78, 118,
  178
Freewriting, 8–10, 31, 43, 50–51, 59, 74,
  78, 105–6, 111, 116, 118, 129, 154,
  157, 178, 181, 188, 198
  focused, 9–10, 20
  timed, 8–9
  unfocused, 20
Freshness, 197–204
Frost, Robert, 98, 115

G

Garrison, Pete, 162
Gossip column, 121
Grahn, Judy, 174, 175–76
Greenberg, Suzanne, 71, 156, 159

H

Hall, Shawn, 83–84
Harris, Evan, 65
Harris, Kevin, 175
Hickman, Shirley, 112–13, 141–42
Hood, Mary, 176
Hughes, Langston, 186–87
Hunigan, Trey, 174, 175

I

Irving, George, 84–85
Ishiguro, Kazuo, 46

J

Jackson, Robert, 27
Jackson, Sarah, 136
Jackson, Selma, 79–80
Jauss, David, 124–25
Jenkins, Charles, 60
Jenkins, Michael, 76, 192, 194
Johnson, Joyce, 117
Jonson, Ben, 201
Journals, 8

K

Kaplan, Rachel, 186
Kaufman, Michael T., 104
Kees, Weldon, 145, 152
Kennedy, William, 183
Klass, Perri, 118, 120
Kornblatt, Joyce Reiser, 68
Kumin, Maxine, 72

L

Language
  clichéd, 205–6
  predictable, 161
Lightfoot, Alison, 166
Listing, 11–12, 34, 38, 39, 44, 47, 50, 54,
  59, 62, 69–70, 82, 98, 102, 106, 116,
  121–22, 126, 129, 144–45, 148,
  180–81, 200

Logbook, uses of, 2–8
Lovell, Mark, 149
Lux, Thomas, 142–43
Lying, 188–90

M

Maher, Kathleen, 137
Mairs, Nancy, 90
Masterson, Rita, 124
McClosky, Judy, 40
McNeal, Alex, 68
Metaphors, 39, 89, 135–37, 161,
     185–86
Mettler, Robert, 71, 204
Miller, Janeen, 178, 179
Moore, Marianne, 57
Morphemes, 164–67

N

Neruda, Pablo, 72
News, creative uses of, 95–97
Nims, Dorothy, 21, 103–4
Notecards, 8
Notes, 66
     absurd, 66
     emotional, 66
     informational, 66, 67

O

Oates, Joyce Carol, 20
O'Brien, Tim, 42
O'Connor, Flannery, 90
Ordan, David, 147, 194
Originality, 197–204
Orlen, Steve, 110

P

Peer review, 197
Pendargast, Bryan, 116–17
Perez, Anita, 96
Petrowski, Arnold, 48–49
Plath, Sylvia, 182

Plumly, Stanley, 80–81
Poems, writing, 21–22
Point of view, 99
Polymorphic words, 165
Predictable language, using, 180
Preferences, exploring changes in,
     154–56
Prefixes, 164–65
Problem solving, 93
Prospecting tools, 8
     brainstorming, 10–11, 20, 26, 30–31,
          58
     clustering, 12, 102, 108–9
     free association, 12–14, 74, 78, 118,
          178
     freewriting, 8–10, 20, 31, 43, 50–51, 59,
          74, 78, 105–6, 111, 116, 118, 129,
          154, 157, 178, 181, 188, 198
     listing, 11–12, 34, 38, 39, 44, 47, 50,
          54, 59, 62, 69–70, 82, 98, 102, 106,
          116, 121–22, 126, 129, 144–45, 148,
          180–81, 200
     puzzles, games, and computers, 14–16
     resistance as a tool, 17–18
     using combination of tools, 19–20
Puzzling crosswords, 14–15

Q

Quigley, Delores, 113

R

Ransom, Karen, 107
Relationships, identifying, 148–50,
     177–79
Repetition, 161
Resistance as a tool, 17–18
Rodriguez, Martin, 109
Roethke, Theodore, 52–53, 150, 163
Romello, Mariam, 178
Root words, 164–65
Ross, Shelly, 65
Russo, Tony, 189

S

Sajé, Natasha, 57
Schaap, Dick, 172
Schwartz, Helen, 51, 52
Seaton, Patty, 28
Sentimentality, 205
Shear, Linda, 170–71
Side effects, 92–94
Similes, 161, 162, 177–79
Simpson, Mona, 63
Slavinski, Frank, 155
Smith, Michael C., 32–33, 61, 91
Smits, Lorraine, 63, 71, 89
Stafford, William, 191
Stories, writing, 22
Subjects, clichéd, 204–5
Suffixes, 164–65

T

Tan, Amy, 171
Tate, James, 29, 36–37
Tension, creation of, 203–4
Thesaurus, computer, 16–17
Thurman, Dave, 186
Timed freewriting, 8–9
Tyler, Anne, 46

U

Unfocused freewriting, 20
Updike, John, 20, 127–28

V

Values, focusing on, 72–73
Verbs, 161, 162
  active, 203

W

Walker, Alice, 20
Wanzo, Haki, 23, 32
Warren, Robert Penn, 20
Washington, James, 101
Watkins, Bill, 63
Weiss, Karen, 56
Williams, William Carlos, 67, 68
Word play order, 161
Words
  arrangement of, 161
  polymorphic, 165
  root, 164–65
Wordstrings, 15–16, 135, 200
Writing
  essays, 22–23
  evaluation of, 197–204
  poems, 21–22
  stories, 22